# SALVAGE STYLE FOR OUTDOOR LIVING

Moira and Nicholas Hankinson

# SALVAGE STYLE FOR OUTDOOR LIVING

Moira and Nicholas Hankinson

RODALE

To Mary Ironside McDonald Gwillim

**RODALE**

WE **INSPIRE** AND **ENABLE** PEOPLE TO IMPROVE
THEIR LIVES AND THE WORLD AROUND THEM

First published in Great Britain 2001 by Kyle Cathie Limited,
122 Arlington Road, London NW1 7HP

Text and designs © **Moira and Nicholas Hankinson**
Photographs © **Tim Winter** except those listed below

**Rodale Organic Living Books**
Executive Editor: **Kathleen DeVanna Fish**
Executive Creative Director: **Christin Gangi**
Project Manager: **Karen Bolesta**
Editor: **Marya Kissinger Amig**
Art Director: **Patricia Field**
Copy Editors: **Sarah Sacks Dunn** and
　　　　　　 **Jennifer Blackwell**
Manufacturing Coordinator: **Jodi Schaffer**
Indexer: **Nanette Bendyna**

**Kyle Cathie Publishers**
Senior Editor: **Helen Woodhall**
Editorial Assistant: **Andrie Morris**
Copy Editor: **Tim Jollands**
Designer: **Kevin Knight**
Production: **Lorraine Baird** and
　　　　　　 **Sha Huxtable**

Color reproduction, printing, and binding by Colourscan, Singapore

**Photo Credits**
Roger Raiche, Planet Horticulture: 8 *center right;* Nicholas and Moira Hankinson: 28, 33 *bottom left,* 34 *left,* 50, 55, 59, 63, 64, 67, 75, 85, 86, 112, 131, 132, 135 *bottom,* and 144

**Library of Congress Cataloguing-in-Publication Data**

Hankinson, Moira.
　Salvage style for outdoor living : beautify your garden using rescued and recycled materials / Moira Hankinson and Nicholas Hankinson.
　　p. cm.
Includes bibliographical references and index.
　ISBN 0–87596–868–6 (hardcover : alk. paper)
　1. Garden ornaments and furniture. 2. Building materials—Recycling.
I. Hankinson, Nicholas. II. Title.
SB473.5 .H26 2001
645'.8—dc21
　　　　　　　　　　　　　　　　　　2001002275

Distributed in the book trade by St. Martin's Press

2 4 6 8 10 9 7 5 3 1 hardcover

Printed in Spain by Artes Gráficas Toledo S.A.U.
D.L. TO: 863-2001

# Contents

An old Gothic-style painted iron bench and an occasionally used iron garden roller nestle below an ivy-clad stone wall and an antique telephone booth from a nearby village.

# INTRODUCTION

In an increasingly affluent society, reclaiming or salvaging old, unused objects or discarded materials such as wood, metal, concrete, or stone just isn't a part of today's busy lifestyle.

But as the indulgent era of the latter half of the twentieth century turns into a less selfish, more caring society, we realize that we cannot "have it all." We want to preserve our architectural heritage, and we hope *Salvage Style for Outdoor Living* will inspire you to rescue and revive the treasures that surround you.

**NEAR RIGHT**

This mixed urn planting features the venerable garden shovel. After years of hard work, it's retired as a sculptural artifact in this California garden.

**CENTER RIGHT**

This simple wooden seat was constructed from a massive plank cut from a hefty wind-blown cypress tree and placed on granite stone supports.

**FAR RIGHT**

This table, made by mosaic artist Candace Bahouth, contains a glorious mixture of seashells, slate, broken tiles, and painstakingly collected colored stones.

At the start of a new millennium, salvaging objects around us makes ecological sense. Too often in the past, proud old timbers were burned for firewood, used bricks were crushed for fill, and weathered roofing slates, battered doors, and ancient windows removed from buildings being refurbished or demolished were discarded as useless, not worth the effort and expense of salvage and restoration. Having no second-hand value, huge quantities of waste material were sent to landfills. Many buildings of architectural excellence were destroyed, and with them much of our past vanished forever.

Change came slowly, fueled by public interest in architectural restoration and the realization that there were commercial opportunities—and indeed large profits to be made—in conserving much of what was previously destroyed. Hence, the traditional building materials and decorative architectural features were gathered to form a unique resource and the inventory of what we now know as salvage or reclamation yards.

In these yards, many glories from our past still can be found—chimney pots and garden statuary, beams, bricks, cast-iron grills and columns, floorboards, flagstones, millstones, paneling and stained glass, and architectural hardware of every description. This vast range of salvaged materials, with its character, color, patina, and texture, reflects the skilled craftsmanship, quality, and attention to detail of artisans from a bygone age.

But back to the present. When the warmer weather arrives, we are tempted to rush to the local garden center and fill our shopping cart with purchases. Such places have proliferated in recent years in response to the seemingly insatiable demand for garden products and plants. There you will see an abundance of standardized stock and rows of concrete reproductions. You may want to purchase some of these, but much of it is best left on the shelf—chances are it is poorly designed, badly made, and quite expensive. Alternatively, for someone who is prepared to invest time and effort, a search through reclamation or

salvage yards, builders' dumpsters, or flea markets and garage sales will reveal a cornucopia of fascinating, unusual, and sometimes ugly objects, which with a little imagination can be used with great effect in the garden.

We are passionate about our subject. The goal of this book is to show how you can incorporate salvaged items into garden schemes. If we jump-start your imagination, we will have been successful. We provide a framework within which you can be inventive, based on an awareness of what is available, keeping component costs low, and using tools that you already own or that are easily obtainable. There are numerous inspirational photographs and 32 different projects grouped together in chapters: "Seating and Retreating," "Plants, Planters, and Planting," "A Garden Reclaimed," "The Themed Garden," "Elements and Ambiance," and "Inventive Ideas." The projects and practical ideas are suitable for all skill levels, whether you are an eager beginner or a dedicated crafter.

We hope that through *Salvage Style for Outdoor Living* you will discover the joy of working with materials others have discarded. When you find yourself hooked on handmade bricks or fall in love with an elegant fountain figure, when your weekends and even your vacations are spent searching salvage yards and construction dumpsters for bits of masonry and snips of metal, when you want to reinvent a use for damaged doors, when your selection of objects is an expression of your taste—you forge a link with the past that still aspires to the future.

**RIGHT**

The shell house in this Mediterranean garden on Tresco island off the coast of England was built from reclaimed materials salvaged from the mainland and the island. Lucy Dorrien Smith decorated the interior of this hexagonal building with mosaic images of flowers, plants, and family monograms.

A hidden corner in a garden room where sitting on an antique steamer chair, sipping a refreshing herbal iced tea, and reading a good book is the height of luxury. Work in the garden takes second place to relaxation on warm summer afternoons.

When the sun shines, the birds sing, and the blossoms are sweetly fragrant, it is time to retreat to the garden and invite family and friends to join in long, lazy lunches that last the

top, adapt a cast-iron sewing machine base to create one of those tables so popular in cafés and pubs, or even convert a huge wooden cable spool into a table.

Alternatively, create an eye-

# SEATING AND RETREATING

whole afternoon or romantic, moonlit supper parties that last well into the night.

To set the stage, create a romantic arbor using sturdy poles as supports in a shaded area—somewhere not too far from the house—and build a barbecue of old reclaimed bricks.

As the focal point of the dining area, construct a table from enormous stones or boulders topped with a slab of slate or flagstone, rejuvenate a sturdy old wooden table by giving it a metal

catching garden detail by making a mosaic-covered table out of seashells collected while combing the beach, or broken tiles and china unearthed while digging in the garden. We used caps from old wooden cheese presses placed on top of slender branches to create tables that have a rustic charm. In contrast, a concrete slab, once the side of a coal bin but now a tabletop on a base of built-up concrete blocks, has more the look of semi-industrial chic!

**NEAR RIGHT**

An abandoned old blue flagstone makes a charming garden seat beneath an arch covered in clematis.

**CENTER LEFT**

This glorious garden playhouse, beautifully proportioned and made of salvaged corrugated iron with cut tin embellishments, stands tall in a city garden.

**CENTER RIGHT**

"The Seat of Conversion" was made by sculptor Paul Grellier from a rescued wayside cross and a variety of salvaged metal and wooden components.

**FAR RIGHT**

The miniature "Little House" is on the grounds of Nigel and Rosalie Dawes' thirteenth-century moated English manor house, Birtsmorton Court. Built of reclaimed lumber, Nigel had it re-erected on the grounds of his medieval house, which serves as a corporate hospitality center.

**ABOVE**

This detail of the garden seat "In Suspension" by sculptor Paul Grellier shows some of the character and color of corroded ancient iron and weathered elm.

**LEFT**

This quiet patio area, which sits high up on a slope and overlooks the garden, has a floor of old clay roofing tiles held in place by a sturdy timber.

Different areas of a garden, like rooms within a home, should generate different feelings. Strategically placed seating provides places to retreat to according to one's mood and adds character to a garden. Make unusual garden seats from sections of cast-iron grills salvaged from an old greenhouse. Use old scaffold boards or pallets or even wood salvaged from windblown trees to make benches, swing seats, or oversized bench tables. Make seats from the stump of an old tree. Cut up old wooden ladders no longer considered safe to make authentic ladderback chairs. Saw old oak whiskey barrels in half for tub seats, or take a timeworn dining chair and plant the seat with your favorite herb. Furnish a sunny arbor with a pine chapel bench. One of our friends even made a seat out of an old cast-iron bathtub cut in half! Why not make yourself comfortable in the garden shed—make a wooden bench on which to perch when you're busy at the potting stand.

Visit historic houses and gardens to see for yourself fine architectural gems and to get ideas. You might be inspired to design and build a garden temple from period salvage, using old floorboards, doors, windows, and shutters to create a glorious hideaway. If building is beyond your budget, let loose your imagination and transform an old tool shed, outhouse, or henhouse, giving yourself somewhere to sit quietly and contemplate. Take your inspiration from nature and make a den, shelter, or a simple retreat.

Inspired by the Romans, grottos were a feature of many landscaped European gardens of the eighteenth century, and you might want to create a grotto of your own. Whatever the size of your garden, a magical space decorated with beautiful shells, planted with shade-loving, large-leaved plants, and enhanced by the soothing sound of trickling water can only add to the atmosphere.

# SCAFFOLD TABLE

## EQUIPMENT

Paintbrush
Tape measure
Tri-square
Pencil or marker
Hand saw
Hammer
Wood chisel
Screwdriver
Drill and wood drill bits
Wrench
Miter saw (optional)
Orbital sander (or coarse sandpaper)

## MATERIALS

Exterior-grade transparent wood
    preservative
Seven lengths of 76-inch scaffold board
    (tabletop and seats)
Four 25¼-inch lengths of 3 x 3-inch
    lumber (legs)
Two 9-inch lengths of 2 x 2-inch
    lumber (seat supports)
3-inch wood screws
Two 60-inch lengths of 3 x 3-inch
    lumber (tabletop supports)
Four 4-inch lag bolts
Two pieces of 8 x 8 x 2-inch
    lumber (braces)
White acrylic paint (or selected color
    of multipurpose paint or stain)

The inspiration for this picnic table came from our stay at a vacation villa in Italy. Dug into the patio gravel, the legs were extended to support a pergola that hosted a glorious shading vine. The table, far longer than the example in this project, soon became the site for lazy lunches and long balmy evenings. A memorable holiday!

Tired of most of the tables so often seen in city parks and picnic areas, we decided to construct a scaled-down version of the Italian original without its roof, large enough to seat eight people but just light enough to be moved around if desired. The table can be made to almost any size, its length extended by joining boards together and adding support frames as required.

If you choose to make a permanent table, the measurement of the legs should be extended to allow at least 8 inches to be inserted into the ground. We used old fencing posts for the frame construction of this table, but rough-sawn lumber can be used instead. Before you begin building your table, measure and record the width and thickness of the boards you will be using—we used scaffold boards that measured 9 x 1¾ inches. This measurement will be useful when you calculate the tabletop and seat heights, normally 30 inches and 18 inches, respectively, and how many boards will be needed for the top.

# SCAFFOLD TABLE

## METHOD

Treat all the wood for the table with the exterior-grade transparent wood preservative. Any cut surfaces should be similarly treated as the construction proceeds.

1 Mark a point 18 inches from the bottom of one of the legs to represent the eventual height of the seat off the ground. Mark a second point the thickness of the scaffold board down from the first point, and a third point 2 inches farther down from the second point. Use the tri-square and pencil or marker to draw horizontal lines across one face at the second and third points. Extend each line by 1 inch across the two adjacent faces of the leg. Join the ends of the two 1-inch lines to mark the area of the leg to be cut out to create a mortise for the seat support. Use the hand saw to cut along the marked sides of the mortise, then remove the wood with a hammer and wood chisel. Repeat this process for the other three legs.

2 Mark the center of one of the seat supports and insert the support into the mortise of a leg. Make sure that the support is centered and that the joint fits tightly. Check that the joint is square and attach the support with two 3-inch wood screws. Repeat with the remaining three legs and seat supports.

3 Before proceeding, lay out the four legs and two frame cross-members on a level surface to familiarize yourself with the construction sequence. Take one of the tabletop supports and use the tri-square to draw a line 3 inches from one end. Mark a point centered between the line and the end of the top support and predrill

a hole for a lag bolt. Repeat for the other end of the tabletop support. Place one end of the tabletop support over the top of a leg, insert a lag bolt into the predrilled hole, and secure it to the leg using the wrench. Secure the other end of the tabletop support to a second leg to complete assembly of the first frame. Make up the second frame with the remaining tabletop support and two legs.

4 Use the hand saw (or miter saw) to cut the two 8 x 8 x 2-inch pieces of lumber in half diagonally to create four triangular corner braces. Be sure the assembled frames are square and attach the corner braces with 3-inch wood screws. If you cannot find 8 x 8 x 2-inch lumber, you can use a brace made from 2 x 2 or 3 x 3 wood with the ends cut at 45 degree angles.

5 Mark the center point of one end of one of the scaffold boards and two points 1$\frac{1}{2}$ inches on either side of the center point. Using the tri-square, draw lines through the second and third points, continuing them around the end onto the bottom of the board to a depth of 3 inches on each surface. Join the ends of the 3-inch lines to create the outline of a 3-inch-square mortise that will fit tightly over the leg. Cut out the marked mortise with the saw, hammer, and chisel. Repeat for the other end of the board and both ends of a second board to create the two bench seats. Place the seats over the seat supports attached to the legs with the mortise fitted over the leg and attach them with 3-inch wood screws.

6 The frame should now be self-supporting. Place it on a level surface and mark the centers of the two tabletop supports and the center of both ends of a scaffold board. Use the marked points to place the scaffold board centrally on the supports and attach it with one 3-inch wood screw at each end. Double-check the angles with the tri-square and secure the scaffold board with two screws at each end. Fit the remaining four boards into place butted on either side of the central board, and the structure of your table is complete. Tighten all the screws to make sure the table is rigid.

7 Paint the entire table with a coat of white acrylic paint diluted to half strength with water; let it dry. (Multipurpose garden paint or stain can be used instead of the acrylic paint, depending on the color finish you want. The Italian table we admired was stained black.)

8 When the paint is completely dry, sand the table with the orbital sander or sandpaper to remove the surface of the paint and reveal some of the underlying wood. Smooth off any rough spots or splinters, paying particular attention to sharp edges and areas where natural wear would occur. The table is now ready to use.

# CHEESE PRESS TABLE

## EQUIPMENT

Wire brush
Rubber gloves
Stiff-bristled paintbrush
Small disposable paintbrush
Tape measure
Wood saw
Garden spade
Hand trowel
Metal or wooden tamper
Hammer

## MATERIALS

Wooden cheese-press followers (caps)
Exterior-grade transparent wood
   preservative
Wood hardener
Logs
6-inch galvanized roundhead nails

## METHOD

1 Take the wooden cheese-press followers, or caps, and remove any soft or extraneous rotten wood using the wire brush. Place the followers on a flat surface and saturate them with transparent wood preservative using the stiff-bristled paintbrush. Make sure the entire surface of the wood is treated, and allow the preservative to soak into the wood. Let the followers dry. Apply a generous coating of wood hardener to the followers with the disposable paintbrush, ensuring that any particularly soft areas are saturated. Again, let the followers dry.

2 Select the logs you will be using for the table stands, which should be at least 8 inches longer than the desired table or seat height. Saw one end of each log straight across. Decide on a location for the tables. For each table or seat, dig a hole at least 8 inches deep where the stand will be inserted, and remove any remaining soil with the hand trowel. Place the post into the hole with the cut end upward and horizontal and replace the soil, firming it with the metal or wooden tamper until the post is held firmly in position.

3 Place each cheese-press follower on the cut end of a post, making sure it is supported in the center, and secure it in place with at least three 6-inch galvanized nails. We selected newly cut willow logs for the table supports, so there is a chance that the willow will root and sprout new growth in years to come.

Safety note

Wear rubber or protective gloves when applying wood preservative or hardener products, which can be harmful. Follow the manufacturers' instructions for application.

Cheesemaking was once an important rural industry. Surplus summer milk was turned into cheese to be used as food for winter and as a vital source of income for the farmer.

Today, cheesemaking is no longer part of twenty-first-century farm life, and old fancifully embellished cast-iron cheese presses can still be snapped up at farm auctions by collectors. The circular wooden press followers, or caps, usually made of elm, are much more common. Made in different dimensions to suit the size of cheese being pressed, these wooden discs were often discarded, their origin unrecognized.

Over the years, we accumulated a number of wooden followers, and we were seeking a practical use for some of the more worm-eaten and less well-preserved discs. Scraps left from the pruning of willow trees gave us the legs to convert our cheese press followers into garden seats and tables.

# CHAIR PLANTER

**EQUIPMENT**

Pliers
Screwdriver
Marker or awl
Metal or tin snips
Metal rule or straightedge
Heavy-duty craft knife
Electric drill and small metal drill bit

**MATERIALS**

Chair with seat rebate
Zinc or metal sheet
1-inch wood screws

Almost any household will have one or two odd or mismatched and unwanted chairs. If not, you can probably find one in local thrift stores or at the roadside awaiting garbage pickup. Seats of many woven or upholstered chairs are removable, and these chairs are ideal for this project. In our furniture design work, we make a number of prototype chairs and the one used for this project is a beech chair that never went into production.

Chairs make effective and attractive planters that can be easily moved around the garden or patio. The one we made for this project is decorative, but we've made others with a sturdier tray support, planted them with fragrant herbs such as thyme or chamomile, and used them as accents in the garden. Any shallow-rooted herb that is suitable for planting in a path or patio can be used, but, because of the planter's shallow tray, frequent watering is essential.

We settled on a simple one-color display for our planter, but a striking effect can be achieved by using plants of different sizes and colors and by embellishing the chair with planted flower pots hung from its back. We decided to make a shallow frame for our chair planter that would be concealed within the seat frame. If you choose to build yours with a deeper tray to hold a greater amount of soil or planting medium, you could fill it with hanging plants to conceal its base.

# CHAIR PLANTER

## METHOD

The chair we selected for this project was neither painted nor treated, and since we designed it for only occasional outside use, we decided to leave it that way. If you want to leave your planter outside, treat the chair with a wood preservative or exterior-grade paint before use. There are a number of attractively colored paints and preservatives now on the market that are ideal for this purpose.

1 Remove the seat from the chair frame and take off any wooden supports using the pliers or screwdriver. Place the chair upside down on top of the zinc or metal sheet on the edge of a work surface, and draw around the inside of the seat with the marker.

2 Measure the depth of the seat mortise and add an extra 2 inches. Draw a second line, the distance of this combined measurement, around the marked shape on the zinc sheet. Trace over this marked line with the awl, creating a slight impression in the metal along the line. Then, turn the sheet over and transfer the line to that side with the marker. Cut the zinc sheet along the second line with the metal snips. Cut a rectangle from each corner from the marked seat size to the outside edge of the zinc sheet using the metal snips, which will allow the zinc sheet to be bent into a tray shape. Draw a line 1 inch from each outside edge. Use the heavy-duty craft knife and metal rule or straightedge to lightly score along the marked line outlining the shape of the seat. Turn the sheet over and score along the second line marked 1 inch from the outside edge. (If your zinc sheet is not large enough to create an entire tray shape inside the seat mortise, like ours in the photos on page 23, create the tray as best you can using the material you have.)

3 Place the zinc sheet on the work surface, with the scored line of the seat shape on top. Gently bend each side of the sheet over the work surface edge to form a tray shape to fit inside the seat mortise. Turn the sheet over and use the work surface edge to gently bend the sheet along the lines scored 1 inch from the outside edge to a right angle, creating a lip around the tray to hold it securely within the seat mortise.

4 Place the completed tray on a piece of scrap wood and use the electric drill and metal drill bit to drill a series of drainage holes in the tray. Then drill two holes in each lip to allow the tray to be securely screwed into position on the seat frame.

5 Place the tray into the seat mortise and secure it in place with two 1-inch wood screws driven through each lip into the seat frame. Fill the tray with soil or planting medium and plant your flowers or herbs. Press down on the soil around the plants and thoroughly water them before placing the planter in position in your garden. You may prefer not to plant directly inside the zinc tray, but to construct a versatile planter that can be used to hold temporary displays of plants in pots. If this is your plan, you will have to build the zinc tray deep enough to hold the pots.

# POTTING STAND

## EQUIPMENT

Paintbrush
Tape measure
Tri-square
Pencil or marker
Hand saw
Electric drill and wood drill bit
Screwdriver
Level

## MATERIALS

Transparent wood preservative
1¼-inch wood screws
2-inch wood screws

## WOOD

For the base:

3-inch-square softwood lumber cut into:
    Two front legs approx. 28 inches
    Two rear legs approx. 44 inches
¾ x 4-inch softwood lumber cut into:
    Two side stretchers approx. 23½ inches
    One rear stretcher approx. 36½ inches
¾ x 9-inch softwood lumber cut into:
    Two bin sides approx. 23½ inches
    One bin front approx. 38 inches
Quantity of approx. 1-inch-square softwood
    lumber (support battens)
½ x 6-inch softwood lumber cut into:
    Two pot boards approx. 36½ inches
½ x 23¾ x 36½-inch piece of waterproof
    plywood or particleboard (bin base)

For the top:

¾ x 8-inch softwood lumber cut into:
    Two side pieces approx. 35 inches
    One bottom shelf approx. 36½ inches
    One vertical divider approx. 23⅝ inches
    One long shelf approx. 24 inches
    One short shelf approx. 11¾ inches
¾ x 9-inch softwood lumber approx. 38½
    inches long (top)
¾ x 6-inch softwood lumber cut into:
    Seven back boards approx. 44 inches

A potting shed can be not only the focus of plant propagating activities necessary for the cultivation of a well-managed garden, but if insulated and properly equipped it also can be a cool retreat in summer and a cozy refuge in winter. Away from the accusing eyes of neglected roses and a vista of unmown grass, it can become a comfortable hideaway for all but the most conscientious of gardeners—a private sanctuary where peace and quiet reign, the demanding shrill of the telephone remains unheard, and the mindless chatter of television and the clamor of much-loved children can be ignored. The perfect environment for indulgence in slow, deep, and somnolent thought.

Unfortunately, such escapism demands a price. A potting shed needs a potting stand to justify the time spent there, and ours is ideal. The bin holds enough compost for almost every job, the shelves accommodate packets of seeds and other tools, and the pot board underneath provides extra storage space. If desired, you can lay a plank or board over the compost bin to create a surface perfect for those other gardening necessities—a book, a cup of tea, or perhaps a glass of wine!

Made from salvaged fence posts and reclaimed roofing softwood, the stand can be disassembled easily and reassembled at a new location, if needed.

# POTTING STAND

**METHOD**

Before assembling the potting stand, paint all the wood you will be using for this project with the transparent wood preservative. Pay particular attention to the cut ends and end grain.

1 Lay one front and one rear leg on a flat surface, the front on the left and the rear on the right. On the top faces of each leg, measure two points 8 inches and 24³/₄ inches from the bottom of the leg. Use the tri-square and pencil or marker to draw horizontal lines at each of these points. Place a side stretcher across the bottom line of both legs and a bin side on the top line and secure them with 2-inch wood screws. Repeat with the other two legs, but this time place the front leg on the right and the rear leg on the left to create the two opposite side frames.

2 Turn the side frames over and fit one support batten to the inside of each bin side, one end flush with and butted against the top of the front leg and the other approximately 1 inch short of the rear leg. Place the two sides upright with their rear legs flat on the surface and the side stretchers and bin sides on the outside. Fit the rear stretcher across the rear legs inside the bin sides, its top level with the top of the battens. Screw it securely in place with 2-inch wood screws.

3 Place the bin front over the front legs, its ends flush with the outside faces of the bin sides, and secure it with 2-inch wood screws. Turn the base over onto its front and fit one support batten to the rear of the bin front between and flush with the tops of the front legs. You have now made the basic structure of the potting stand base.

4 Stand the base upright on its legs and, checking that the frame is square, fit the two pot boards over the side stretchers, butting them against the back legs. Attach the boards with 2-inch wood screws.

5 Carefully measure the inside dimensions of the open-backed bin you've made and cut the waterproof plywood or particleboard to that size, removing a notch from each back corner to fit over the rear legs. Drop the board into place so that it rests on the battens, the front legs, and the top of the rear stretcher, and secure it with 1¹/₄-inch wood screws. The potting stand base is now complete.

6 You are now ready to start building the potting stand top. First check the measurement between the outsides of the rear legs of the base. Depending on the thickness of the lumber you have used for the base construction, this should be approximately 36¹/₂ inches. This measurement is important because the top is designed to fit snugly over the rear legs (which are raised above the top of the base) and rest on the bin sides. Measure a point 10¹/₄ inches from the bottom of each side piece and, using the pencil and tri-square, draw a line across each side piece. Fit the bottom shelf between the two side pieces level with that marked point and secure it to the sides with 2-inch wood screws. Take the top piece and place it on top of the side pieces with an overhang at the sides and front and secure it with 2-inch wood screws. You have now constructed the basic frame of the top. Mark a point 11³/₄ inches from one end on both the top piece and the bottom shelf. Fit the vertical divider at that

point with 2-inch wood screws to divide the frame into two unequal sections. Mark points just above the halfway point on the inside of the vertical divider and side piece within the wider section and fit the long shelf in position, securing it with 2-inch wood screws. Finally, mark points approximately 1¹/₂ inches above the long shelf on the inside of the remaining smaller section and secure the short shelf at that position with 2-inch wood screws.

7 Place the assembled top structure face down on your work surface, check that it is square, and, starting at one side with the edge of the first back board flush with the outside face of the side piece, proceed to attach the remaining back boards to the rear, securing them with 2-inch wood screws. You may have to cut the final board to fit. Carefully lift the completed top section onto the base so that it fits over the extended back legs and the side pieces rest on the bin sides. Secure it with 2-inch wood screws driven through the back boards into the legs and the rear edge of the bin sides. Place the potting stand into position, fill the bin with potting soil or compost, and it is ready to use.

# CONCRETE TABLE

## EQUIPMENT

Pointing trowel
Shovel
Cement-mixing board or wheelbarrow
Level
Tape measure
Mallet
Soft brush
Paintbrush (optional)
Large sheet of plastic

## MATERIALS

Soft or builder's sand
Water
Cement
Approximately ten 6-inch concrete blocks
Concrete slab top
Multipurpose garden or masonry paint
(optional)

## METHOD

If you're building the garden table on a solid surface, clean the surface of any lichen or other growth. At a new site, build the table on a concrete foundation (1 part cement to 2 parts soft or builder's sand and 4 parts aggregate) at least 12 inches deep. The foundation should be allowed to harden before the base is installed. Calculate how many blocks will be required to construct a base of the right height for the table. Standard tabletops are approximately 30 inches high. Remember to allow for the thickness of the tabletop and each layer of mortar.

1 Place two concrete blocks approximately ³/₄ inch apart on the ground where the table base will be built. Draw around them with the point of your trowel and put the blocks to one side. Make up a workable mortar mix of 5 parts sand to 1 part cement and water and place a thick layer of the mix inside the trowel marks. Replace the two blocks in position on the mortar and tap them into place with the handle of the trowel, periodically checking with the level. Clean off excess mortar from around the base and use it to fill the joint between the two blocks. Do not fill the gap completely, as this may cause the blocks to splay.

2 Place the next two blocks perpendicular to the first course. Apply mortar across one end of both blocks on the first course sufficient for one of the blocks on the second course. Tap the block into place, checking that it is level and that the sides are vertical. Place mortar on the remainder of the first course and lay the fourth block alongside the one you have just laid. Fill the outside of the vertical joint and smooth it.

3 Continue building up the base to the desired height, checking with the level as you go. To fit the top, place mortar around the edge of the top course and a trowelful in the center. Fit the top carefully on the mortar, and when it is centered, make sure it is level. Tap it firmly in place with the handle of the mallet. Remove excess mortar from around the top of the base. After about 4 hours, brush over the joints with a soft brush to remove any loose material. Keep new blockwork moist in hot weather and protect it from sun, wind, rain, or frost with the large sheet of plastic. Allow 1 week for the mortar to cure before using the table. If desired, the base can be painted with two coats of multipurpose garden paint or masonry paint applied with a stiff paintbrush.

Alfresco dining is one of life's great pleasures. While portable tables can be taken into the garden for an impromptu occasion, a properly designed permanent table can be convenient and extremely useful. Before you build a permanent table in your garden or on your patio, we suggest you erect a temporary mock-up in the proposed location to make sure the site is suitable. Once built, it will be a lasting feature.

During inclement weather the table can be used to display arrangements of plants in pots or urns, or for an outdoor sculpture. It will become a focal point of the garden, as much appreciated when not in use as when it is the venue for outdoor entertaining.

Finding a tabletop of a suitable size can be a problem. Tabletops can be made of wood or even heavy glass, but we made this one from the side of an old concrete coal bin that was no longer in use. It was extremely heavy, requiring at least two people to move it, and we had to fill the bolt holes in its corners with a sand and cement mixture. However, it was very sturdy, and its beveled edge made it particularly suitable as a tabletop. Large stones, slate, or concrete paving slabs are other alternatives for garden tabletops.

An arrangement of salvaged stone bases, an old stone trough, ancient bricks, a slate slab, various clay and terra-cotta pots, and artful planting create a peaceful haven.

It's so easy to drive down to the local garden center, load up the shopping cart, and buy containers for your garden—as easy, in fact, as going to the supermarket for your weekly food shopping. Although there is always a good selection of mass-produced pots, trays, and planters to choose from at a variety of prices, the one thing they lack is individuality. So next time you are tempted to jump into the car and run to the garden center, stop for a moment and think about what you already have lying around that could easily be recycled.

Check in the garden shed, look at the back of the garage, and even investigate the unsightly pile at the front of the house awaiting a trip to the garbage dump. Put aside old terra-cotta piping, metal buckets, concrete blocks, and wooden packing cases—in fact, anything that looks as if it could contain plants or shrubs and withstand having holes drilled in it for drainage. You'll be astonished at just how many items you already own that can be recycled into objects that are useful, decorative, and add new color, texture, and shape to your garden.

# PLANTS, PLANTERS, AND PLANTING

Container gardening is advantageous, particularly where restricted space limits the number of plants that can be accommodated. Planters can be easily moved around, repositioned if the plants need more light or shade, or built up on supports to give the display height and structure. Planting in containers allows a garden to be changed with the seasons—species intolerant of cold can be grown outside to provide color through the summer and then brought inside with the approach of colder weather.

Raised beds are often used to grow neat rows of cabbages, lettuce, chard, and other vegetables together with swirls of sage, parsley, and thyme. They answer the problems posed by limited space and are useful if you want to grow acid-loving plants in a lime-rich garden. Raised beds allow the soil to heat up faster, are easily maintained, and can be constructed from a wide choice of materials, including old lumber, which looks informal and can be found in the classified section of the newspaper or at reclamation dealers.

Paint an old, bottomless metal bin an old-fashioned dark green or other subdued color to blend with your plants, or choose primary colors of red, blue, and yellow just for a bit of fun! Transform salvaged oil drums, large wooden bins, metal feed troughs, cans, and cast-iron gutters with bright paint colors. Painting adds an instant, easy, and inexpensive effect that will lift your spirits and add life to a boring backyard.

Create wooden tubs from whiskey and wine barrels, attach shapely legs from old cast-iron bathtubs to the base of an old boiler—even the wire baskets from a long-unused freezer make ideal planters. Transforming these utilitarian but sometimes ugly objects into eye-catching containers can be quite a challenge, but with some thought and a little effort, they can be turned into interesting and unusual planters.

### FAR LEFT

A carved stone feeding trough in the garden of a retired farming couple was once in use in the cattle yard of their former farm. Eight men were needed to carry it to the garden of their present home. Old stone troughs are in great demand and fetch high prices at garden antique auctions.

### CENTER LEFT

An ancient brick door leads to productive kitchen gardens. The terra-cotta urns and bases blend perfectly with the old mellow brick wall.

### NEAR LEFT

An established wisteria has been trained to grow on supports made from lumber salvaged from discarded wooden pallets and mounted on a stone wall facing a kitchen window.

### BELOW LEFT

Tripod legs have been secured to a weathered log to make a rustic plant stand used to conceal an unsightly drain cover in this urban garden.

### BELOW RIGHT

Old slate is used as edging to retain a bed of flowering culinary herbs beside this lush kitchen garden.

### LEFT

A typical wood-framed farmhouse in Normandy, France, has its gable end adorned with a glorious mix of summer flowers in a variety of salvaged containers.

# BUCKET PLANTER

## EQUIPMENT

Scrubbing brush
Bucket
Electric drill
Wire wheel or sanding flap disc

## MATERIALS

Galvanized metal container
Liquid soap
2 wooden wedges
Liquid metal polish
Medium-grade steel wool
Soft cotton rag

## METHOD

1 Remove all wrapping and any string or labels attached to the bucket.

2 Wash the bucket thoroughly with the scrubbing brush and hot soapy water to remove surface dirt and grime. Let it dry.

3 Place the bucket on its side on a work surface and wedge it in place with the two wooden blocks to keep it from moving while you are working on it. Use the electric drill and wire wheel and/or the sanding flap disc to remove surface oxidation and discoloration from the bucket. When you see the wheel or disc begin to mark the galvanized coating, proceed with caution because you don't want to cut through this coating to the underlying steel.

4 Work over the surface of the bucket in a circular motion with a wad of the steel wool dipped in the liquid metal polish. Keep the steel wool saturated with the polish and change it when it starts to lose its ability to cut into the surface of the bucket. Work on a small area at a time, periodically wiping the surface clean with the cotton rag to inspect the finish until all the scratch marks produced by the wire wheel or sanding flap disc have been removed and the bucket is bright and clean.

Since this planter is not perforated for drainage, we've placed it under the overhang by our back door, where it is protected from the rain but can be watered when necessary. It is important not to overwater your plants. Many plants can suffer as much damage from water saturation as from drought. Our galvanized metal planter is the perfect complement to the blue stone paving on which it stands.

Even basic galvanized metal containers can be transformed into attractive and useful garden and patio planters.

The container we selected for this project was a former army bucket, one of thousands that were produced after World War II. Discovered in a surplus yard piled shoulder-high with similar buckets, the protective but now rotten cloth cover was removed to reveal the army logo and the date February 1952 embossed in the metal.

Like many articles produced for government use, this bucket was made to precise standards. After 30 years of storage and 20 years of neglect stacked outdoors, the heavy galvanized coating, although dull, tarnished, and stained, protected the underlying metal from rusting. The galvanizing was as effective now as it was when the bucket was first made.

The shape of the bucket suggested a planter, and we felt that to show it at its best, we should remove some of the surface oxidation and reveal the color and patina of the underlying galvanized coating.

Most galvanized steel can be cleaned using a similar method to ours, but remember some modern galvanizing may not have as thick a coating as our bucket. Use a gentle hand when cleaning such objects.

# PACKING CRATE PLANTER

**EQUIPMENT**

Claw hammer
Pliers
Wood saw
Scissors
Staple gun and heavy-duty staples
Craft knife

**MATERIALS**

Wooden packing crate
Scrap lumber or plywood
1-inch paneling nails or thin nails
Quantity of fine-mesh garden netting
    or burlap
Potting soil or planting medium
Selection of plants

The current demand for ceramic pots, vases, and bowls has resulted in innumerable fragile vessels being imported from all corners of the world, many packed in wooden boxes or crates to protect them during their travels. We've found these crates to be a ready and inexpensive source of sometimes quite exotic timbers. We used a crate that was made of wooden branches lashed together with rawhide to make a stunning coffee table base. We salvaged Brazilian mahogany that was used to pack machine parts to construct tabletops and benches.

Keep your eyes open for discarded materials that can be salvaged and transformed into something surprising and exotic. The packing cases we found for these planters were discovered in a well-known store. Used to hold glazed pots, they were about to be put out with the shop's trash. The store manager was only too glad to let us take them away.

Disposal of unwanted packaging is an increasing problem for retailers, and they are generally very willing to let you simply have it. Damaged or broken pallets are an excellent source of lumber, and by being willing to sort and collect it ourselves, we seldom have to purchase new boxes or packaging for the furniture that we make and sell.

# PACKING CRATE PLANTER

## METHOD

1 Place the packing crate on a solid surface and remove the lid and any protruding nails or staples using the claw hammer and pliers.

2 Turn the crate upside down. Cut pieces of the scrap lumber or plywood to fill any gaps in the bottom of the case. Secure the wood pieces with the paneling nails or thin nails to make a solid floor for the planter.

3 Cut the fine-mesh garden netting or burlap into four pieces to match the shapes of the sides of the inside of the box. Use these pieces to line the interior of the planter, attaching with the staple gun and staples.

4 Fill the packing crate planter halfway with potting soil or planting medium. Using the scissors or craft knife, cut Xs through the garden netting at places where you want plants to grow sideways through the planter. Gently insert the plants through the netting and into the planting medium. Complete the planting from the top of the case. We planted a selection of culinary herbs in this planter, but almost any plants can be used. Water the plants well and, when drained, place the planter in its selected location. If you want, you can convert this planter into a hanging basket by attaching screw eyes and a length of chain to each corner of the packing crate.

# CAST-IRON TUB PLANTER

## EQUIPMENT

Wire brush
Electric drill and high-speed metal drill bit
   (optional)

## MATERIALS

Copper or cast-iron tub
Chimney pot

## METHOD

1 Clean the copper or cast-iron tub with the wire brush to remove any extraneous rust. Similarly, use the wire brush to clean the chimney pot of any cement or mortar and unsightly stains. If you want to plant directly into the tub, at this stage you will have to use the electric drill and high-speed metal drill bit to make a drainage hole in the tub's base, but since we chose to insert a potted plant into the tub, this was unnecessary.

2 Place the chimney pot in position, making sure that it is vertical and the top is level. Carefully place the tub on top of the chimney pot, taking care not to chip the top of the chimney pot while centering the tub. Check the final height of the planter—we decided to put an extra piece of stone under the chimney pot to raise the planter. Plant as desired or place a potted arrangement inside the tub.

There are many locations in almost any garden where a fixed planter can be placed. We covered a long-abandoned well in front of our house with a stark and unsightly stone slab that now dominates what was once a vegetable garden but is now lawn. We looked for a simple architectural element that would mask this stone and add a touch of drama to the garden. We experimented with a sundial but decided the area needed something else. A simple yet striking tall planter seemed to be the perfect solution and, having no other ideas, we decided to visit a local reclamation yard to seek inspiration.

Copper tubs are frequently in demand and expensive to buy, if you are fortunate enough to find one. However, the much more common cast-iron tub was once a feature in almost every home and the focus for the thriving domestic activity that surrounded the weekly family wash. We found our cast-iron tub among a number of others in the salvage yard, and nearby there were some old chimney pots, any one of which could have been used for this project.

# WASTEBASKET PLANTER

Tape measure
Pencil
Ruler or straightedge
Wood saw
Hammer
Electric drill with small wood drill bit
Screwdriver
2-inch paintbrush

## MATERIALS

Quantity of marine- or exterior-grade
    plywood
1-inch paneling nails or thin
    roundhead nails
Quantity of approximately 1-inch-square
    softwood lumber
1½-inch wood screws
Dark brown wood preservative

## METHOD

Our wastebasket was constructed of slats of wood fixed to a rigid wood framework and was designed to hold a removable metal or plastic liner that had long disappeared. Otherwise, the bin was in an excellent shape.

1 Measure the inside dimensions of the four sides of the wastebasket and use the pencil and straightedge to draw their shapes onto the marine- or exterior-grade plywood. Cut the shapes from the plywood using the wood saw and attach the shapes inside the bin using the paneling or roundhead nails.

2 Measure the depth of the plant container you will be placing inside the wastebasket and add approximately 2 inches to that measurement to give you the depth at which to fix the battens inside the bin. At that depth, measure across the inside of the wastebasket and cut two battens to that length from the 1-inch-square softwood lumber. Use the wood screws to fit the two battens on opposite sides of the interior of the bin.

3 Measure the width across the wastebasket at the battens and cut three or four slats from the 1-inch-square lumber to fit. Start holes with the electric drill and wood drill bit and secure the slats in place on the battens with the wood screws. Paint the entire planter with a liberal application of the wood preservative, allow it to dry, and then place the plant container on the slatted support inside the wastebasket.

We discovered this wooden wastebasket in our local recycling center. The bin was discarded and its metal liner was missing, but its shape suggested a new life as a chic patio planter. We soon discovered a second matching wastebasket, this one complete with a plaque proclaiming "Place Litter Inside," which we quickly removed and installed on the door to our teenage daughter's bedroom.

Large planters are essential for large plants and lavish planting schemes, and these wastebaskets were perfect for the site and plants we selected. Their construction is so simple that we subsequently made up several more in different sizes for a townhouse patio garden.

The original wastebasket was aged and very faded, and we decided to spruce it up with a coat of wood preservative. You can also finish such bins with a transparent wood preservative if you want to retain the original look, or you can transform them by adding a coat of colored wood paint or preservative.

# TIRE PLANTER

**EQUIPMENT**

Wire brush
Garden spade

**MATERIALS**

Old car tire
Can of multipurpose spray paint

**METHOD**

We selected a fairly small car tire for this project because we wanted to restrict the growth of the ornamental rhubarb. You may want to stack a number of similar-size tires to create a forcing tower for your plant.

1 Using the wire brush, clean the outside surface of the tire. By removing any mildew, dirt, or fungus and any loose or flaking rubber, you will provide a smooth surface for painting.

2 Lay the tire flat and spray the outside and top of the tire with the multipurpose spray paint. We recommend using a spray paint rather than painting the tire with a brush because it is easier to get complete coverage with the spray, particularly inside the tire tread.

3 Place the tire on the ground in the position it will be installed and mark the inside hole edge using the point of the garden spade. Remove the tire and dig or loosen the soil inside the spade mark to a depth of at least 12 inches. Add some mature compost to the hole, plant the ornamental rhubarb, and return the tire to its position, over the plant. Never plant food crops inside tires, which can leach chemicals into the surrounding soil.

Managing large amounts of discarded tires is an increasing environmental problem. As the number of cars on our roads increases, the tires that are used and discarded also rises. Some scrap tires are burned in incinerators to generate power, while others are ground and used in asphalt highways, artificial reefs, and a number of other products.

We've seen old tires used in numerous inventive ways in gardens around the world, and one of their most appealing uses is as planters for ornamentals. While you may not consider automobile tires to be an attractive addition to a garden, they can be a practical solution where space is at a premium.

It is said that gardens and gardening are good for the soul, and many a city dweller craves his or her own piece of private outdoor space. However small—whether it is a roof terrace, a patio just big enough for a barbecue, or a balcony decked with potted plants—it is somewhere to toil with a trowel in the open air or an essential sanctuary in which to just sit and think. The trend toward outdoor living has been fed by a plethora of garden makeover programs created for television. As a result, instant gardens fashionably furnished with wooden decks, terra-cotta pots, and architectural, foreign plants have climbed to the top of the must-have list for many people. In reality, gardens are not instant creations but evolve over time and need care, however low-maintenance the design may be. If at any time the garden is redesigned, the plan will usually incorporate many of the existing plants, shrubs, and trees.

# A GARDEN RECLAIMED

**ABOVE**

An informal arrangement of
nineteenth-century damaged
terra-cotta pots is almost
overwhelmed by succulents.

**RIGHT**

This superb example of an
original Victorian greenhouse
was rescued from dereliction
by John Nelson and reerected
at The Lost Gardens of
Heligan in Cornwall, England.

In this chapter, we've taken a small garden that was neglected and transformed it, working as much as possible with what was already there. As parsley, fennel, and a border of piercing, purplish blue catnip were already established in the garden, they made an obvious starting point from which to establish a fragrant herb garden that would be sweetly scented on summer evenings, provide some greenery all year round, and yield delicious herbs for cooking. In our design, the herb garden enclosed a crazy-paved area that used stones salvaged from the garden and that was softened by more herbs growing between the slabs. Still more herbs were planted into a few clay drainage pipes (pots also could be used) to achieve extra height and structure. Reached by four stone steps edged with wooden timbers, the design incorporated various edgings of terra-cotta and slate tiles, wooden blocks, and old mellow bricks, with slate chippings and tiny pebbles used as mulch.

We added two other essential features—the soothing sound of water and a table for alfresco dining. We bought an old cattle water trough and painted it dark green, creating an

ideal container to blend with the garden plants. The trough was filled with water and an inexpensive fountain pump was placed inside, along with striking yellow irises found abandoned on the roadside after ditches had been cleared. We built a table using the concrete side of a coal bin as the top and concrete blocks as the base.

Before the garden came to fruition, much groundwork needed to be done. The soil had to be excavated and several loads disposed of, revealing a stony substructure and a lot of trash. This was nothing compared to the garden that we acquired with our rundown farmhouse, which, once tilled, produced enough fragments of stones, flint, broken terra-cotta, baling twine, colored plastic, old bones, rusty metal, decomposing leather, shards of glass, and china chips to fill an entire abandoned quarry.

It was the bits of broken china that first caught our eyes. The blue-and-white patterns we found were commonly used for everyday dinnerware. We became fascinated, or perhaps we should say obsessed. A journey to the compost heap or wash line was impossible without eyes glued to the ground in search of treasure. There was a joy in finding tiny pieces of china in shades of blue, ranging from pale pastels through bright cobalt to inky blacks, large pieces and small, all caked in grime. Eventually, the collection filled three empty shoe boxes. One day in the dim and distant future, when time allows, we'll use the pieces to cover the concrete table, making a magnificent mosaic.

# BRICK EDGING

## EQUIPMENT

Pointing trowel
Garden spade
Shovel
Cement-mixing board or wheelbarrow
String and pegs
Level
Soft brush
Large sheet of plastic

## MATERIALS

Quantity of old bricks
Broken stone
Cement
Soft or builder's sand
Aggregate

## METHOD

Carefully select the bricks you'll use for this project. Since they will be laid on edge, ensure that at least one edge is sound and remove any extraneous mortar with the pointing trowel. If you are using different colored bricks or the sizes vary slightly, mix them well before laying them in order to achieve a uniform appearance. Put aside any mortar removed from the bricks and add it to the broken stone to be laid in the base of the trench.

1 Excavate a trench 10 inches deep the entire length of the proposed edging border. Fill the trench with a 4-inch layer of compacted broken stone. On the mixing board or wheelbarrow, use the shovel to make a dry mixture of 1 part cement to 3 parts soft or builder's sand and 6 parts aggregate. Cover the stone base with the dry mix to a depth of about 4 inches. Using the string and pegs to create a straight line, lay the bricks on their edges on the dry mix approximately ½ inch apart. Tap the bricks firmly into the bed of dry mix with the handle of the trowel and check that they are level.

2 Make another dry mix, this time with 1 part cement to 4 parts sand, and use it to fill the joints between the bricks, removing any excess mortar with the soft brush.

3 Cover the bricks with the large sheet of plastic to protect them from rain, and let them set for at least 7 days for the mortar mix to take up moisture from the soil and atmosphere until it completely hardens. By using a dry mix to lay the bricks, you will minimize any mortar spills and cement stains.

Old bricks are probably the most commonly reclaimed building material. Usually known as "old stock" bricks, they are required for much of the construction work in areas where new buildings must match the existing architecture. Although old bricks are readily available, they require some cleaning to remove old mortar before they can be reused.

Old bricks have a charm, individuality, and character lacking in their modern counterparts, with colors ranging from blue (almost purple) to yellow and hardness ranging from the granite-like density of some stable bricks to the soft crumbly texture of many low-fired handmade stocks. Despite their attractiveness, most old bricks from demolition sites are still taken to landfills because the labor required to sort, clean, and find a market for them outweighs their commercial value.

Brick is an obvious and practical solution for garden edging, and the bricks we rescued proved ideal for this project.

We are active dumpster-watchers, always keeping our eyes open for usable materials. We recently retrieved a large number of bricks from restoration work being done on a local department store. The bricks, mostly in excellent condition, were being loaded into a dumpster before being taken to a landfill, and the site foreman was more than happy to allow us to remove those bricks that we wanted to salvage. (Always be sure to get the builder's permission before removing anything from a construction dumpster.)

# RAILROAD TIE AND STONE STEPS

## EQUIPMENT

Tape measure
Chain saw or crosscut saw
Garden spade
Shovel
Wheelbarrow
Cement-mixing board or wheelbarrow
Mallet
Bolster or stone chisel
Wood scrap
Level
Large sheet of plastic
Pointing trowel
Soft brush
Watering can with fine rose

## MATERIALS

Quantity of paving stone
Quantity of railroad ties or timbers
Large quantity of broken stone
   or rubble
Cement
Sharp sand
Aggregate

Safety note

When using a chain saw, wear full face protection,
protective clothing, and a dust mask. Also wear
eye protection when cutting stone with a mallet
and bolster or stone chisel.

For years, the only access to our raised garden had been an agile leap from some old stone steps at the end of a path, which had once led to the adjoining property, onto a pile of concrete blocks and from these onto the garden, which was about 3 feet above the level of the path. This was not a practical arrangement, especially when carrying home-grown produce or a watering can and garden tools.

Steps leading from the path to our new patio garden were desperately needed. Steps must be both practical and safe. Their width may be dictated by the site, and their number by the height and the material you will be using for the risers. We were fortunate to have a number of short lengths of railroad ties, given to us by a neighboring farmer and which we had left over from various other garden projects. We wanted the steps to blend with the colors and textures of our garden, so we decided to make the treads of our steps with paving stone to match the existing stone retaining walls of the raised garden.

Because railroad ties can leach dangerous chemicals, do not use them where you will grow food.

# RAILROAD TIE AND STONE STEPS

## METHOD

When selecting the stone you will use for this project, look for stones of similar size and depth and make sure each stone has at least one good surface. Reject any that are flaking or crumbling. Measure the width of the steps you will be building and cut the railroad ties to that length with the chain saw or crosscut saw. Be sure to wear a mask and gloves when working with treated wood.

1 Select a quantity of paving stones of approximately equal size and depth sufficient to cover the proposed tread area of the steps and put them to one side. The height (rise) and depth (tread) of the step will be dependent on whether you propose to use the ties on edge or flat. Normally the rise should be 6 to 8 inches and the tread should be twice that measurement. Calculate how many steps will be required by dividing the height of the slope where the steps are to be built by the measurement of a single riser. Dig out the first step to the dimension of the tread, but excavate a further 6 inches at the front as a footing on which the railroad tie will be laid.

2 Fill the bottom 4 inches of the footing with compacted broken stone or rubble. On the cement-mixing board or in the wheelbarrow, make a mortar mix of 1 part cement to 4 parts sharp sand and sufficient water to make a firm mix, and use it to cover the broken stone in the footing to a further depth of about 2 inches. Lay a cut railroad tie on the mix, tap it into place with the mallet, and make sure it is level. Cover it with the large sheet of plastic to protect it from rain and let it set for at least 24 hours. When

dry, fill the excavated space behind the riser with more compacted stone and rubble to within approximately 4 inches of its top. Make another batch of mortar mix, but this time dry (without water). Place the dry mix over the compacted stone, and place the paving stones into it so that their surface is level with the top of the railroad tie riser.

3 Lay each paving stone down with a screwing motion to ensure that it is securely bedded and will not rock or move, adding or removing dry mix as required. Try to keep the gaps between stones as small as possible—if necessary, the paving stones can be cut to size with the mallet and bolster. Use the hammer cushioned with a scrap of wood to tap the stones into place. When the paving is laid and leveled to your satisfaction, use more of the dry mortar mix to fill the joints. Press down the mixture between the joints with a scrap of wood to compact it, and use the soft brush to clean off any debris and surplus dry mortar mix from the paving surface. The dry mix will normally take up moisture from the soil and atmosphere, but in dry weather you can sprinkle water from a watering can fitted with a fine rose, covering it with the large sheet of plastic, and letting it set.

4 Repeat the above steps for each rail tie and stone step, ensuring that the level of the top of the last riser is finished flush with the proposed level of any new paving or surface. To construct the steps for our raised garden, we built a retaining side wall of reclaimed stone. We used a mortar mix of 1 part cement to 1 part soft sand and 4 parts stone dust. We used the stone dust in order to match the mortar used on the existing walls. The appearance of newly constructed steps can be softened by planting a few lime-tolerant, low-growing plants in soil-filled crevices created during construction.

# STONE CRAZY PAVING

**EQUIPMENT**

Garden spade
Shovel
Wheelbarrow
Level
Board or plank
String and pegs
Wood scrap
Cement-mixing board or wheelbarrow
Mallet
Bolster or stone chisel
Medium-bristle broom
Soft brush
Watering can with fine rose
Large sheet of plastic

**MATERIALS**

Quantity of paving stone
Large quantity of broken stone
 or rubble
Cement
Sharp sand

Safety note

Always wear eye protection when cutting stone
with a mallet and bolster.

Our raised garden was the result of generations of former occupants depositing their household and farm trash on the land. For the first few years after we bought the farmhouse, we used the garden for growing vegetables and in the course of digging found fascinating evidence of the past. Shards of blue-and-white willow pattern crockery are now stored for future mosaics; remnants of salt-glazed pots and buckles from discarded harnesses told of earlier times; and on one occasion we even unearthed a brass cartridge case. Although this area was fertile, we felt it was wasted space since it was made redundant by a new kitchen garden. We decided to turn the raised garden into a paved sitting area facing west, which would allow us to enjoy the last evening light.

We live in an area where most houses are built of stone, and the aggregate used widely throughout the region for pillars and gateposts and the local blue lias flagstone are particularly in demand. Built on the site of a considerably older farmhouse, many of our outbuildings predate the house. A consequence of such extended occupation is the large amount of stone and other building materials found all over our garden hidden just under the soil.

Among the stone we've recovered from our garden is a considerable quantity of paving stone, some of which was used for this project.

# STONE CRAZY PAVING

**METHOD**

Before you begin, make sure you have an adequate supply of reasonably large paving stones to cover the area you want to pave. Select stones of equal depth and make sure that one face of each stone is smooth. Put aside stones that have one straight edge to be used as edge pieces.

1 Remove any weeds and debris from the area to be excavated, taking particular care to remove any roots.

2 Excavate the whole area with the garden spade and shovel to a depth of approximately 6 inches plus the average depth of your paving stones. Compact any loose soil and check that the area is almost level using the board or plank and the level. Allow for a slight slope for drainage.

3 If you've decided to border the paved area with garden beds or to create a complex shape, tie the string to the pegs and drive the pegs into the ground to mark the edges. Continue excavating the area to the string line. Remove all of the excavated soil from the area to be paved. Later, you may want to add this soil to your borders.

4 Fill the bottom 4 inches of the excavated area with broken stone or rubble, and use the wood scrap to compact it. On the mixing board or in the wheelbarrow, use the shovel to mix a dry mortar of 1 part cement to 4 parts sharp sand. Spread the dry mix over the broken stone to a depth of about 2 inches. Starting from one corner, lay the edging pieces first with the straight edge outward. Add interior stones until the area is covered. Make sure all the stones are securely bedded, adding or removing dry mix as required. The gaps between the stones should be small; if necessary, cut the interior stones to fit using the mallet and bolster.

5 When the paving stones are laid to your satisfaction, sprinkle the dry mortar mix over the paved area and use the broom to brush it into the joints. Compact the mortar between the joints with the wood scrap and use the soft brush to clean off any excess mortar from the surface. (In wet weather, the dry mix will take up moisture from the soil and air. In dry conditions, sprinkle water from a watering can fitted with a fine rose.) Cover the area with the large sheet of plastic to protect it from rain and let it set.

# EDGING SLATE AND TILES

## EQUIPMENT

Electric slate and tile cutter
Garden spade
String and pegs
Wood scrap
Shovel
Cement-mixing board or wheelbarrow
Soft brush
Pointing trowel
Level
Mallet
Watering can with a fine rose
Large sheet of plastic

## MATERIALS

Quantity of broken slates and tiles
Broken stone
Cement
Soft or builder's sand
Sharp sand
Aggregate

Safety note

Wear eye protection and a dust mask when using electrical cutting equipment.

Old tiles and slates (along with reclaimed bricks) are the life blood of most salvage yards. The variety of color found in native and imported slate is almost bewildering, and the range of sizes and patterns which tiles were made in the past means that matching old tiles can be quite difficult and time-consuming.

We've used slates and tiles in our garden for all sorts of purposes and have seen them used in numerous inventive ways in other gardens around the world. Old slates are an obvious choice for roofing garden structures, but they can also be used to cap a wall or to act as a hard-wearing flooring material. We use them buried deep into the soil to contain invasive plants in a border. Laid on edges we show in this project they have a particularly attractive appearance. Tiles are just as useful. We know of one enterprising gardener who built an entire garden bench from stacked double Roman tiles. In the same garden, tiles were laid to delineate paths and beds.

In almost any reclamation yard, you will find discarded and broken tiles or slates that can very often be had for the asking. There is something particularly satisfying in securing a useful material for nothing! We decided to make a border of mixed edging for our raised herb patio garden and managed to construct it entirely from old and broken slates and tiles from a local reclamation yard.

# EDGING SLATE AND TILES

**METHOD**

Since the slates and tiles will be laid on edge in this project, make sure you have enough for the job. You will need approximately 8 tiles or 16 slates for each 6 inches of edging. Select slates and tiles at least 6 inches long by at least 4 inches wide. Use the slate and tile cutter to trim the pieces to a uniform length. The width of the slates can vary between 4 inches and 6 inches because this edge will be hidden below the surface of the ground.

1 Using the garden spade, dig a trench approximately 10 inches deep the entire length of the edging area. Tie the string to the pegs and insert the pegs into the soil at each end of the edging to act as a guide for laying the slates and tiles. Fill the trench with the broken stone to a depth of approximately 4 inches and use the wood scrap to compact it to form a firm base.

2 On the cement-mixing board or in the wheelbarrow, use the shovel to make a dry mixture of 1 part cement to 3 parts sharp sand and 6 parts aggregate. Spread the dry mix over the broken stone to a depth of about 4 inches. Lay the tiles on edge and about $\frac{1}{2}$ inch apart in the dry mix in the trench. Lay the tiles in alternate blocks of eight laid at right-angles to each other—first a block of eight across the trench, then a block of eight laid lengthwise, and so on.

3 Make up a second mortar mix, this time of 1 part cement to 3 parts soft or builder's sand and 1 part sharp sand. Use this mix to fill the gaps between the tiles, removing any excess mortar with the hand brush. Tap the tiles level with the handle of the trowel, using the level to ensure accuracy.

4 Repeat steps 1 and 2 to lay the slates in the trench where required. The gap between the slates will be less than that used for the tiles, and it will be easier to lay them across the width of the trench rather than lengthwise. Slates are quite fragile, so if you need to tap them into the dry mix, use the handle of the trowel or the mallet cushioned by a piece of scrap wood.

5 When the edging is completed, check it with the level. Ideally, the surface of the edging should be just above that of the earth to be retained behind it and flush with any paved or other surface abutting it. While the concrete and mortar mixes are still dry, use the club hammer with a cushion of scrap wood to gently tap the slates and tiles into their final position.

6 Cover the newly laid edging with the large sheet of plastic to protect it from rain and let it set for at least two days to allow the dry mortar to take up moisture from the soil and harden. (In particularly dry weather, sprinkle water over the finished edging with a watering can fitted with a fine rose before covering with the plastic.) Finish by laying any paving or other surface up to the edging.

# RAILROAD TIE EDGING

## EQUIPMENT

Chain saw or crosscut saw
Disposable plastic tarp
Old paintbrush or household brush
String and pegs
Shovel
Cement-mixing board or wheelbarrow
Sledgehammer
Cement trowel
Level

## MATERIALS

Selection of railroad tie scraps
Exterior-grade transparent wood
    preservative
Quantity of broken stone
Cement
Sharp sand
Aggregate
Soft or builder's sand
Water

Safety note

Wear protective clothing, a dust mask, and full
face protection when using a chain saw.

Old railroad ties have become the ubiquitous yet essential raw material for almost every television garden makeover program or newspaper article on restoring a garden produced or written over the last few years. Invaluable for building casual steps or for terracing a sloping garden, railroad ties have been used for many purposes in our garden, and we've accumulated a stockpile of scraps.

We used some scraps on end as paving for a patio and others as stepping-stones in a wild area of the garden. We decided that a number of them could be usefully incorporated as one of the variety of different edging materials we planned to use in our new raised patio garden. Because old railroad ties can leach dangerous chemicals, do not use them where you will grow food crops.

The railroad ties used in different parts of our garden were secured from a variety of sources, and some were quite rotten. We trimmed the ties to size for this project, and we treated some of the scraps with a preservative before using them.

# RAILROAD TIE EDGING

**METHOD**

Be sure to wear a mask and gloves when working with treated wood.

1 Use the chain saw or the crosscut saw to cut the railroad tie scraps into equal-length blocks (approximately 10 inches). Make sure that at least one end of each block is relatively solid and square.

2 Lay the blocks on the tarp. Using the old paintbrush or household brush, saturate the blocks with exterior-grade transparent wood preservative, making sure that the newly cut ends are covered. Let the blocks dry completely before continuing.

3 Tie the string to the pegs and place the pegs in the soil to mark the proposed position of the edging. Dig a trench along the string at least 10 inches deep. Line the base of the trench to a depth of approximately 3 inches with the broken stone. Make a dry mixture on the cement-mixing board or in the wheelbarrow of 1 part cement, 3 parts sharp sand, and 6 parts aggregate. Lay this mixture in the trench to within approximately 3 inches of the ground surface.

4 Make another mixture of 1 part cement to 4 parts soft or builder's sand and water as needed and lay it on the dry concrete mix. Place the blocks in position on the wet mortar mix approximately $1/2$ inch apart, leaving the tops approximately 3 to 4 inches above ground level. Fill the gaps between the blocks with the wet mortar and smooth it with the trowel. Use the string and pegs to check the alignment of the blocks and the level to check that they are level, making any necessary adjustments with the club hammer or handle of the trowel.

These winding stone steps were constructed with old paving stones found beneath layers of ancient asphalt.

Using color as a theme on which to base a garden design—whether it is in the hot spectrum of reds, yellows, oranges, and pinks or the cool blues, greens, purples, and violets—will

Japanese, African, or Australian gardens in the heart of the city! Gardens built around a water theme—from formal fountains to fish ponds—are extremely popular and can be found in the

# THE THEMED GARDEN

certainly draw the eye and make a visual impact as it saturates the garden with corresponding hues from spring through late summer to autumn.

Visit any of the major garden shows in any large metropolitan area and you will find unexpected pleasure in discovering

backyards of suburban homes and small city townhouses alike. Lush desert gardens can be created using fragrant desert lilies, prickly cacti, and spreading yuccas, while a tropical theme can revolve around soaring palm trees, Adam's-needle, and delicate white gaura blossoms.

### ABOVE

"In Memory of Everlasting Soles," an unfinished garden sculpture by Paul Grellier, features old iron shoe forms and a salvaged churchyard plaque mounted on a stone base.

### TOP RIGHT

Reclaimed bricks and stone were used throughout this beautiful English garden.

### OPPOSITE LEFT

The formality of this garden pool edged with reclaimed stone pavers is offset by the simplicity of the lawn and the yellow flag irises.

### BOTTOM RIGHT

This wooden seat hidden in a secluded garden corner was made from stone supports rescued from an old church and original nineteenth-century terra-cotta pots.

### OPPOSITE CENTER

Antique stones once used to grind corn make an interesting garden detail.

### OPPOSITE RIGHT

The shallow, lichen-covered steps leading down to this pond were made from old coping stones rescued from a demolished garden wall.

Other themes that make strong statements are herb, rock, and wild gardens. Important natural habitats for birds, animals, and insect life, wild gardens can include woodland areas and can be home to masses of wildflowers and lush green ferns. Take it one step further and a woodland garden can become a jungle overflowing with palms, giant gunnera, bamboo thickets, and numerous exotic trees, shrubs, and marsh plants.

Moving from natural wilderness to more formal gardens, sculpture and other props can be used to great effect as focal points. Place statuary stone lions, dogs, birds, and deer beside ornate urns and vessels that have been stacked on stone bases to create a gallery, adding a touch of grandeur to even the most modest of outdoor spaces.

Containers provide an instant visual effect, whether they are wooden tubs on a terrace or terra-cotta pots on a patio. Metal tubs, dustbins, and old galvanized florist's buckets look particularly striking when planted with clipped trees or topiary shrubs and silvery

foliage. If this look is not to your taste, old-fashioned metal buckets can be planted with a variety of greenery or flowering plants to create a more informal appearance. Enjoy the richly aromatic fragrance of herbs basking in the warmth of sunlight by planting rosemary, thyme, parsley, sage, chives, marjoram, bay, basil, coriander, and mint in buckets outside your back door.

The sensuous sound of water flowing in the garden—trickling, rushing, gushing, and cascading—brings about a feeling of serenity, soothing away the tension and anxiety that builds up in our daily lives. Electricity, which we take so much for granted, allows us to take power to the farthest corners of our gardens, letting us create artificial waterfalls and fountains. A rectangular, square, or circular pool of water, which may be home to koi, carp, or goldfish, can be a formal feature in the garden; a wildlife pond, home to flora and fauna such as water lilies, dragonflies, frogs, and toads, has a more informal, natural appearance.

Whichever theme or combination of themes you choose for your garden, wood will play an essential role. Contrasting superbly with natural foliage and materials like stone, slate, brick, and terra-cotta, wood can be used both structurally and decoratively. You can create boundaries with attractive picket fencing made from discarded pallets or transform railroad ties into sweeping steps leading to borders flanked with heavenly scented lavender bushes or attractive lady's mantle to soften the hard edges. In perennial gardens, railroad ties make practical raised beds for foxglove, butterfly weed, and globeflowers.

Teak is a hardwood that is very popular for garden furniture because it is long lasting and fades to a glorious gray color. A softwood hexagonal table that we found in a garden nursery and that was once used to display stock was reborn in a buttercup meadow, its surface planted with turf and ready for a summer picnic—romantically ephemeral and wonderfully surreal!

# RAILROAD TIE STEPS

## EQUIPMENT

String and pegs
Tape measure
Chain saw or crosscut saw
Paintbrush
Garden spade
Shovel
Pickax
Level
Mallet
Hand saw
Hammer
Electric drill and wood drill bit
Plank or board for leveling
Wheelbarrow
Garden rake

## MATERIALS

Selection of wooden railroad ties
Exterior-grade transparent wood
    preservative
Lengths of softwood approx.
    1 x 8 inches
Dark brown wood preservative
3-inch galvanized nails or screws
Quantity of ½-inch screened and
    washed paving gravel

Safety note

When using a chain saw, wear protective clothing,
full face protection, and a dust mask.

Ever since the introduction of concrete railroad ties, old hardwood ties have been a valued resource for garden designers who want a long-lasting raw material for construction work.

Railroad ties can be bought at almost any reclamation yard or garden center, but some of those used have been "double reclaimed," first from the railways and subsequently from local farmers. While not in perfect condition, the ties we used were so saturated with oil and preservative that large parts of them could be salvaged.

There are many different ways to build steps within a garden. For this gentle slope, alongside a converted pigsty finished in reclaimed wood, we chose to use crushed stone gravel retained behind a step made from the base of a demolished old stone wall already on the site and hardwood railroad ties.

Because of the preservatives in railroad ties, make sure you use them only where they won't come into contact with soil where you grow any edible vegetables, fruits, or herbs.

# RAILROAD TIE STEPS

**METHOD**

Mark out the area to be excavated for the steps using the string and the pegs. Bearing in mind that the top of the gravel layer will be flush with the top of the railroad ties, work out how many steps are required by measuring the drop from the top to the bottom of the slope and dividing this by the height of a single step—each step should be no higher than approximately 8 inches. (We decided to lay our railroad ties on edge rather than flat in order to match the height of an old stone wall base we were incorporating as one of the steps and to limit the number of ties required.) Cut the ties with the chain saw or crosscut saw to the proposed width of the steps. Treat the cut ends with exterior-grade transparent wood preservative and let them dry.

1 Steps look better and are easier to climb when they are constructed an equal distance apart. Starting at the top of the steps, use the spade (and, if necessary, the pickax) to excavate a trench for the first railroad tie. Lay the tie in the trench, checking its alignment with the level and making sure that at least 3 inches of the tie is buried in the ground for stability.

2 Continue excavating and laying the railroad tie steps until all are in place. Make sure that the ends of the railroad ties are in line so that when the wood edging is fitted, the sides of the steps will look neat and even. Use the mallet to bed the ties firmly and secure them in place with compacted soil and stones, checking the horizontal and vertical alignments periodically with the level.

3 For the edging, cut pieces of the 1 x 8-inch softwood to the distance between each step. Make sure that each piece is long enough so that its ends, when fixed in position, fall in the center of the ties. Apply the dark brown wood preservative to the softwood pieces, making sure to saturate the cut ends. Set them aside to dry. Using the level to check the alignment, fix the softwood edging in position between each step with the galvanized nails or screws. When nailing near the end of a cut edge, predrill the nail hole to prevent the wood from splitting.

4 When the steps and their edging pieces are completed, excavate the soil from the area to be covered by gravel to at least 2 inches below the top of each retaining railroad tie. Compact the excavated area to form a level surface on which to place the gravel, using the level and the plank or board to check for accuracy. Add the gravel, using the garden rake to spread it level and flush with the top of the railroad ties. The gravel will settle over time, so make sure you have enough on hand to top the steps off at a later date.

# WATER GARDEN

### EQUIPMENT

Stiff wire brush
Paintbrush
Face mask
Level
Paint scraper or hook

### MATERIALS

Old steel cattle trough (or other suitable
    water tank)
Black marine-grade paint (make sure it is
    safe for pond use)
Red oxide metal primer paint
Spray can of multipurpose outdoor paint
Electric fountain (or water pump)
Silicone caulk sealant

Safety note

Electricity is extremely dangerous, especially if
used in or close to water. Use only UL-approved
equipment specifically manufactured for outdoor
and underwater use and get expert advice before
connecting it to the main power supply. Special
outdoor fittings and wiring are essential for
outdoor use or damp conditions. Electric shocks
received from incorrectly fitted or inappropriate
equipment, particularly when used in the presence
of water, can cause serious injury or even death,
so don't take chances. Seek advice from a
qualified electrician.

Water gardens have become very popular—with good reason. Running water adds the dimensions of sound and movement to a garden, and the presence of water—whether running or still—will lure wildlife to a garden, attracting numerous birds, animals, and insects, all requiring a year-round supply of drinking water.

Water can add a focal point to a garden as well as offer the gardener an opportunity to grow a whole new range of plants. However you choose to add water to your garden, read up on the subject and consult a local expert retailer about the various plants you can use and which, if any, fish to purchase. Because fish need oxygen to survive, it is important that your water garden contains oxygenating plants or that some mechanical device is used to keep the oxygen in the water at the correct level.

Farmers often stock the cattle troughs in their fields with goldfish, perhaps won at a local carnival or fair. The fish help to keep the troughs clean of insect larvae and other impurities. Our old but serviceable cattle trough, purchased at a farm auction, was incorporated into our paved garden using a small and inexpensive fountain to aerate the water and to provide the garden with sound and movement.

# WATER GARDEN

## METHOD

When choosing a trough or tank for this project, make sure that the metal is solid, without holes or perforations. Troughs that have a hole or fitting near the top for the old water supply are ideal because the hole will provide a concealed entry for the fountain's power cable.

1 Scrub the trough vigorously with the stiff wire brush to remove any rust or loose and flaking material. Clean the trough inside and out, paying particular attention to the base, which might be in contact with the ground when installed and therefore may be especially prone to rust.

2 Turn the trough onto its side and brush out any remaining loose material or rust debris. Apply two coats of the black marine-grade paint to the inside of the trough up to the level of any access hole or, if none exists, to within approximately 2 inches of the top. Make sure the entire surface is well covered. Let it dry.

3 Apply a coat of the red oxide metal primer paint to those parts of the trough, inside and out, not covered by the black marine-grade paint. Let it dry completely, then apply a second coat and let it dry.

4 Apply one or two finishing coats of the multipurpose outdoor paint over the red oxide primer. We chose to use a spray paint to get an even finish, but similar paints can be applied by brush. Always use a face mask when spray painting and follow the manufacturer's directions.

5 Position the painted trough in its final location. Once it is filled with water it will be extremely heavy, so make sure it is exactly where you want it to be, checking its alignment with the level. (We chose to raise our trough onto four bricks rather than set it on the ground, which can encourage rust.) Fill the trough with water to the top of the marine-grade paint, ideally using rainwater (although you can use tap water).

6 Thoroughly read the installation instructions that accompany the fountain or water pump. Feed the electric cable through the trough's access hole, if one exists, or pass it over the top of the tank into the water and place the fountain in position. It may be necessary to raise the fountain onto stones or bricks so that it is at the correct level in the water. If desired, you can drill a hole into the tank just above the water level for the electrical supply and seal the hole with silicone caulk sealant. (Please see the safety note on page 76. It is very important that the fountain and the power supply are checked before the power is turned on.) Once this is done, plant your trough with water plants, turn on the fountain, and enjoy the ambiance that trickling water creates.

# METAL BUCKET PLANTER

Electric drill and ¼-inch metal drill bit
Paintbrush (optional)

## MATERIALS

Old metal bucket
Black marine-grade paint (optional)
Metal lacquer (optional)
Selection of stones or broken
    terra-cotta pots
Potting soil or growing medium
Plants

## METHOD

1 If your bucket has no perforations in its base, drill a number of holes to provide drainage and to prevent the soil from becoming saturated.

2 If desired, paint the inside of the bucket with the black marine-grade paint and the outside with a coat of the protective metal lacquer to preserve the appearance of the metal and to help prevent corrosion. Fill the bottom 2 to 4 inches of the bucket with broken pot shards or stones to allow free drainage to the drilled holes in the base. Add the potting soil or growing medium to the bucket and place the plant in position, firming the soil around it.

Zinc and other metal planters and containers are enjoying a resurgence in popularity in the garden. Our commitment to reusing old materials has led to our making planters from old bread tins and dustbins, garden edging from corrugated-iron strips, arbors from metal reinforcement rods, and numerous garden arches from scraps of steel concrete-reinforcement sheets.

Planters created from rusty, old, battered, and sometimes perforated metal buckets can be far cheaper than purchasing modern metal containers. Old or discarded buckets, when grouped together and fully planted, make an attractive display on a set of wide steps or a patio.

Many of the buckets we've used had rusted to such an extent that no drainage holes were necessary. If this is not the case with your bucket, be sure to perforate the base to provide adequate drainage.

# RAISED BED

## EQUIPMENT

Tape measure
Chain saw or crosscut saw
Four scaffold boards or planks
Garden spade
Level
Board for leveling
Mallet
Claw hammer

## MATERIALS

Two 10-foot railroad ties
Quantity of 6-inch galvanized
   roundhead nails
Screened garden soil, compost, or
   growing medium
Exterior-grade wood preservative

**Safety note**

When using a chain saw, wear protective clothing,
full face protection, and a dust mask.

A raised bed is one of the most productive uses of a small growing space. Ideally, the bed should be constructed to a size that can be worked without the need to walk on it. Once established, the raised bed should never again require deep digging. All cultivation, composting, planting, weeding, and harvesting can be carried out from the sides and ends, and because it's never compacted, the soil will remain crumbly and easily worked. No wonder the raised bed is sometimes known as a "lazy" bed.

A properly established and managed raised bed allows closer planting than is normal and will produce a greater yield than can be obtained in most ordinary garden beds. The raised bed in this project was constructed from 10-foot railroad ties. In order to minimize waste, we decided to lay the ties on edge and cut them into 6-foot and 4-foot lengths to create a bed that would allow easy access to any point within the bed.

Raised beds can be constructed from many different materials. We've seen them made from brick, stone, concrete blocks, old wooden palettes, and even raised earth banks, but railroad ties are ideal for this particular application.

Because of the danger of creosote and other preservatives leaching into the soil, plant only ornamental plants in any garden you construct using old railroad ties.

# RAISED BED

**METHOD**

1 Cut each railroad tie into a 6-foot and a 4-foot length with the chain saw or crosscut saw. Treat the cut ends with the exterior-grade wood preservative and roughly assemble them on flat ground in the shape of the proposed bed. Measure the outside dimensions of the assembled bed, including the railroad ties. Lay the 4 scaffold boards or planks on the ground where the bed will be dug to outline a space of the measured dimensions.

2 Using the garden spade, dig a trench the width of a railroad tie around the perimeter of the space outlined by the boards to a depth of at least one-third the height of a tie, which will be set below the surface of the surrounding soil. Use the level and a board to check that the base of the trench is level.

3 Lay one of the longer ties in position in the trench. Tap it into place with the mallet, making sure that it is securely bedded, and check that it is level. Carefully lay one of the shorter end ties at a right angle to the longer tie. Bed down the end, ensuring that the tops of both ties are level and that their ends are butted tightly together. Using the claw hammer, nail the ties together with two 6-inch galvanized roundhead nails driven in at an angle from the top of the ties at each side of the joint.

Repeat this step with the remaining railroad ties, making sure that the corners are square and the tops of the ties are level. When all the ties are in place, dig the soil inside the newly created bed to at least one and preferably two spade depths, incorporating screened garden soil, compost, or growing medium to bring the final soil level up to just under the top of the ties. This is the perfect time to remove any stones or weeds from your soil. When the bed is dug before planting, try not to walk on or compact the turned earth because this is when you will create the loose soil structure that is one of the main benefits of a raised bed.

# GRASS-TOP TABLE

## EQUIPMENT

Old paintbrush
Pliers, wire cutters, or heavy-duty scissors
Staple gun and staples
Sharp knife or craft knife
Garden sieve (optional)

## MATERIALS

Slatted wooden table
Exterior-grade wood preservative
Wire netting
Large sheet of plastic
Quantity of sod
Sieved soil (optional)
Water

## METHOD

Any slatted table can be used for this project. Alternatively, a solid table will work if it is perforated with enough holes to provide adequate drainage. If the table selected has no retaining edge, construct one out of exterior-grade softwood lumber, nailed or screwed to the edge of the table to provide a lip of at least 4 inches.

1 Treat the entire table with the exterior-grade wood preservative, paying particular attention to end grain, the legs where they will be in contact with the ground, and the tabletop and lip into which the soil and grass will be placed. Let the table dry.

2 When the preservative is completely dry, cut the wire netting with the pliers, wire cutters, or heavy-duty scissors to the shape of the tabletop and attach it with the staple gun.

3 Cut the large sheet of plastic (we used an old tarp) to fit the tabletop and perforate it for drainage. If the lip is deep enough, spread a layer of approximately 4 inches of soil over the entire surface. Lay the sod on the soil or plastic liner, cut the pieces to shape with the knife, and press them firmly into place, making sure the joints between the sod pieces are tight in case of shrinkage. Water the tabletop thoroughly and keep it moist so the grass does not dry out. In autumn, spring bulbs can be planted between the grass and the underlying soil to provide a stunning spring flower display. If you are planning to picnic on your grass table, make sure you never use any pesticides or other chemicals to treat the grass.

Every so often you come across something that you know is just too good to miss! Such was the case with this wooden plant display table that we bought for a song at a garden nursery auction. Once home, the table sat outside, adding to the debris of what has become our very own reclamation yard. We knew that one day we would find a use for it.

Early one morning, we awoke to the sound of what we thought was thunder until, looking out of the window, we saw a herd of cattle gamboling like overgrown lambs on our lawn. After 5 months of being penned in during the winter and smelling the lush green grass of our precious lawn, the cattle had broken out and proceeded to turn our lawn into what looked like a tank training ground or the aftermath of a rock festival.

After several weeks and a few visits from grim-faced insurance adjusters, the outdoor maintenance crew came to relay the lawn. One week later, we had a new expanse of bowling-green quality lawn and several pieces of sod left over from the job. Inspiration struck. Why not plant our table with the sod and create a year-round garden attraction?

We planted the sod straight into the existing shallow recess of the table. To extend the life of the sod, lay it on a base of compacted soil at least 4 inches deep.

A stone balustrade,
salvaged from a once
grand but since
dilapidated house, is now
installed in the new
Mediterranean garden,
one of the themed areas
within the Abbey Gardens
on the English island of
Tresco.

Long ago, the only elements in the universe were thought to be earth, water, air, and fire. In today's garden, the elements are the structures, textures, colors, plants, props, and light that help formed; and parterres and topiaries were established. Lakes and ponds were designed to blend into the countryside, interrupted only by a hidden sunken fence. Today, few of us can change the

# ELEMENTS AND AMBIANCE

to create an ambiance and personalize the area.

The great landscape designers of the past created amazing vistas by altering the natural landscape to fit an invented plan or scheme. Tree planting was undertaken on a massive scale; formal structures with large sweeps of manicured, terraced, and walled gardens were physical characteristics of our gardens. We have to live with and work around what is already there, usually on a minute scale compared with great estates. With monotonous regularity, we clip the hedges, mow the lawns to perfection, weed the borders, and deadhead the roses in an effort to achieve a neat, tidy, and well-managed garden.

**ABOVE**

Water pours from an old brass faucet into a reclaimed stone trough in a lovely water garden.

**RIGHT**

Massive stone pillars support beams cut from storm-blown trees to create an oversize pergola supporting long-established kiwifruits and passion flowers.

There is a group of people who have become bored with rows of box hedges, who are reacting against symmetry, who no longer want to force flowers and plants to grow in conditions that are the very opposite of their natural habitat, who, in short, feel we should all stop fighting nature and work with it instead. These same people find the smoke, gasoline fumes, and noise pollution of the lawn mower antisocial and believe that conventional gardening involves too much destruction of the natural environment. This movement favors a looser style of lush planting for the twenty-first century, accidental-looking drifts or expanses of shape, color, and texture. Emulating nature, they advocate mixes of grasses, perennials, herbs, self-seeding annuals, fruits grown at random, and spontaneous mixes of wildflower meadows. Of course, nothing is ever quite that easy. This style of gardening and planting requires skill to make it look as if it has just happened—and it needs a degree of control to avoid a hodgepodge look. But the timing is right for this style. It is part of the organic, environmentally friendly trend with which we are comfortable.

### LEFT

This view from a stone bridge looks across a moat at the entrance to a walled garden. The wrought-iron gates, lead planter, and stone steps were installed during restoration work on the property.

### BELOW LEFT

Old stone slabs salvaged from a farmhouse are surrounded by ancient cobblestones and then bordered with an edging of reclaimed clay roof tiles to make a path through this kiwifruit-shaded pergola.

### BELOW RIGHT

This informal pond—a haven for wildlife—is bridged by an old railroad tie, entirely in keeping with the mood and colors of this part of an exciting garden.

If you yearn for the flower-filled fields and meadows of your childhood—much of it now swallowed up by housing developments—do not despair. There is no reason why a scaled-down wildlife reserve can't be planted in a backyard or clumps of graceful grasses freely cultivated on a balcony or even in a window box.

This freedom of expression is at odds with designers who fill gardens with bold concepts in concrete, metal, and glass with only the occasional nod toward the token plant. If you find this controlled style both cold and ugly, look to where your pleasure lies.

Perhaps you have a fleeting image of an evolving space whose structures are a succession of textured brick walls, gentrified cobblestones, gnarled and knobbly wooden fences, and glorious slate terraces in hues of grey, blue, black, and heather. Perhaps you see worn, wooden summer houses laced with an air of mystery, their ancient windows of uneven glass, and pathways of muddy brown stone and shingle. Linked by a natural theme of scents from flowers and herbs, sounds from birds and insects, and the distant gurgle of water, our gardens—whatever their design, colors, or textures—are a haven of refuge, offering us a kind of spiritualism that seems to be missing in many of our daily lives.

# GLOVE STAND

## EQUIPMENT

Craft knife
Electric drill
Selection of spade bits

## MATERIALS

Large, heavy piece of wood with one flat
  side
Selection of firewood branches
Sandpaper
Waterproof wood glue
Transparent wood preservative or
  furniture wax (optional)

## METHOD

Choose the wood you will use for this project carefully, ensuring it is dry and well seasoned. The large, heavy piece of wood with one flat surface will be the base. Select a number of fairly thin, similarly sized straight branches for the uprights.

1 Use the craft knife and the sandpaper to remove any bark from the branches and sand them to a smooth finish. Cut the branches to a uniform length. Round off the top (smaller) end of each upright with the sandpaper.

2 Trim the bottom (larger) end of each upright with the craft knife and sand them to a uniform tapered shape.

3 Using the electric drill and spade bit, cut a hole for each upright in the base piece. Drill each hole at a slight angle from vertical so that when the uprights are fitted into place they will splay out at an angle.

4 Apply waterproof wood glue to each hole and fit the uprights firmly into position. Check the splay and put the completed stand to one side to dry. If desired, finish the stand with an application of transparent wood preservative or furniture wax.

What do you do with your canvas gardening gloves when they are not in use? Where do you keep the leather pruning gauntlets when they are damp? And where are they anyway? However neat the garden room or potting shed, the multitude of gloves needed for the various jobs around the garden have a habit of getting mislaid or hiding themselves in some dark and dusty corner.

In an attempt to tackle this problem, we've come up with a storage stand for the many different garden gloves that gardeners seem to own—a simple stand that will store damp gloves and allow them to dry properly, an object that is both functional and pleasing to look at.

We live in an area where willow trees line every stream and ditch, and farmers must trim and prune them on a regular basis. Not only do we enjoy a constantly changing landscape, but we also enjoy an abundance of smooth, sturdy branches, the perfect resource for our project.

# GARDEN LIGHT

**EQUIPMENT**

Orbital sander or sandpaper
Tape measure
Hand saw
Electric drill and wood drill bits
Screwdriver
Pencil or marker
Straightedge
Paintbrush

**MATERIALS**

Wood-framed stained-glass window
Glazing putty (if necessary)
Length of 1 x 1-inch wood (battens)
Quantity of 2-inch wood screws
Length of 1 x 8-inch planed
    wood (sides and base)
Multipurpose outdoor paint

When daylight has dwindled, nighttime dining outdoors by the soft light of candles is particularly pleasurable. You can purchase a bewildering selection of electric outdoor lights at any garden shop or discount department store, but we prefer the warm glow from lamps and the flickering light of candles. For special occasions, we have candles in hurricane glasses on tall metal spikes that we insert into the grass and borders, and tea lights in antique Victorian glass containers and small faceted tumblers. We own several old paraffin lamps bought at farm auctions, and we have made numerous candle holders from old farm and garden tools, staircase spindles, and clay ink bottles found at flea markets.

Asked what they find difficult to sell, salvage dealers say the small stained-glass windows removed from late nineteenth and early twentieth-century houses, for which there seem to be few alternative uses. Easy to find and inexpensive to buy, we thought these windows could be simply converted into garden lights that would cast an attractive diffused glow through their patterned glass. We've used stained glass windows to make many of these lights and also to cover recessed wall lights. We even inserted one window into the gable end of a garden shed to cast patterned shafts of colored light onto an otherwise boring interior.

# GARDEN LIGHT

**METHOD**

1 Use the orbital sander or sandpaper to remove any loose or flaking paint from the window frame. It's not essential to remove all of the paint, but it is important to provide a smooth surface for painting. Replace any putty that is missing from the front of the window.

2 Turn the frame onto its front and measure its height. Cut the 1 x 1-inch wood into two battens, each approximately 1½ inches less than the height of the frame. Predrill screw holes along the length of each batten and attach them to the rear of the frame 1 inch from each outside edge, using the 2-inch screws. (The distance the battens are fitted inside the edges of the frame will depend on the thickness of the lumber you are using for the sides. Measure your lumber and adjust this dimension accordingly.) The battens should be attached approximately 1 inch from the bottom and ½ inch from the top of the frame.

3 Place the 1 x 8-inch planed wood on the work surface and make sure its end is square. (If you are using wood such as an old floorboard, you will probably need to cut the end off in order to discard any damaged wood.) Mark a point equal to the height of the frame along one edge of the piece of wood. Mark a second point approximately 1 inch less on the opposite edge of the piece. Join the points with the pencil or marker and the straightedge and saw along the line. Using this angled cut end as a pattern, cut a second identical side piece from the remainder of the wood.

4 Place one of the cut side pieces onto the back of the frame and butted against the batten with the angled end toward the top and the taller edge to the front. Predrill screw holes and attach the side piece to the batten with at least three 2-inch wood screws, making sure not to insert any screw within 1 inch of the bottom. Repeat with the other side piece.

5 Measure the distance between the side pieces assembled on the window frame and cut another piece of the 1 x 8-inch planed wood to that measurement to form the base. Attach the base to the frame using 2-inch wood screws driven through the predrilled holes in the side pieces. The assembled light should now be able to stand without additional support.

6 Paint all the wood surfaces with multipurpose garden paint and let it dry. Then place a candle inside a secure metal or other fire-resistant container behind the stained glass, and the garden light is ready to use.

# SLATE MEMO BOARD

**EQUIPMENT**

Slate cutter
Paint scraper or palette knife
Selection of different grades
    sandpaper or emery paper
Electric drill and ¼-inch drill bit
Block of scrap wood
Paintbrush (optional)

**MATERIALS**

Selection of old roofing slates
8-inch length of leather bootlace or strip
    of scrap leather for each slate
Matte or satin finish exterior-grade
    varnish (optional)

**METHOD**

1 The size of the memo board will depend on the slate available, but this is a good way to use smaller or broken slates. Slates are normally hand split and cut to create one beveled edge and one flat edge. The slate cutter is designed to produce a similar cut edge. Before cutting your project slates to size, we recommend you experiment with the cutter on scrap slate to familiarize yourself with how it cuts.

2 Use the paint scraper or palette knife to remove any flaking or delamination to reveal the sound surface underneath. Use the sandpaper or emery paper to sand the slate smooth, starting with a coarse-grade paper and finishing with a fine-grade paper to achieve the best finish. Place the slate on the piece of scrap wood with the beveled edge up and, using the electric drill and ¼-inch bit, drill a hole through the slate centered about 1 inch from the top of the slate. Drilling through the slate into the scrap wood will minimize any risk of the slate breaking while the hole is being cut.

3 Feed the leather shoelace or strip of scrap leather through the hole, tie the two ends into a simple knot, and the memo board is ready to hang from a hook or nail—the perfect wall ornament for the garden room or potting shed. If desired, the slate surface can be sealed with a coat of matte or satin finish exterior-grade varnish.

Slate has a lovely appearance and an interesting texture. Plus, it is one of the most versatile of all salvaged materials, having multiple uses throughout the home and garden. In this book, we show you how salvaged slate can be used to make garden markers (see page 116) and edging (see page 60), and in the chapter "A Garden Reclaimed" (see page 47), we illustrate how broken and chipped slate, collected from a salvage yard, can be used as a very effective and attractive garden mulch. Old slates can be used to isolate invasive plants, such as mint, in an herb bed and as tiles on the surface of a stone or wooden table. You can sometimes get scraps from thick slate that was cut down to make flooring slabs and kitchen work surfaces from flooring contractors, and use it to make an imposing path edge.

Reclaimed roof slates are easy to cut, and if they are heavily delaminated or flaking from exposure to the elements, they can be converted into invaluable place mats, memo boards, and clipboards for the home and garden. In this project, we show you how to make a stylish slate memo board, but the project can be easily adapted to create a clipboard by fitting a bulldog clip to the top of the slate to hold a paper pad.

When writing with chalk on a slate board, wet the chalk first. This will ensure that your writing stands out when the chalk has dried.

# TOOL RACK

## EQUIPMENT

Tape measure
Carpenter's square
Pencil
Hand saw
Straightedge
Jigsaw (optional)
Electric drill
$1^1/_2$-inch hole-cutting bit
1-inch wood chisel
Wood drill bits to fit screws
Screwdriver

## MATERIALS

Selection of lumber:
   2 pieces approx. 1 x 10 x 43 inches (top and
   base)
   2 pieces approx. 1 x 16 x 36 inches (sides)
   1 piece approx. 1 x 6 x 43 inches (rear)
Selection of approx. $2^1/_2$-inch wood screws

## METHOD

1 Lay out the two pieces of the 1 x 10 x 43-inch lumber. On the length of one face of each piece, mark a line approximately 2 inches from each long edge using the pencil and the straightedge. Starting 2 inches from one short end of each piece, mark points at 8-inch intervals on each line so you have two rows of five marks. Select one board as the top and drill holes through the plank at the marked points using the electric drill and hole-cutting bit. On the second board, which will be the base, drill holes with the hole-cutting bit at the marked points, but only to a depth of approximately $^1/_2$ inch. Remove the cut wood with the wood chisel to create a recess in which the tool handles will eventually sit.

2 On one short end of each of the two 1 x 16 x 36-inch pieces of wood, mark a point 10 inches from one long edge. Using the pencil and the straightedge, draw a line from the 10-inch marks on an angle along the same long edge of the planks to the corner on the other short end. Use the hand saw or jigsaw to cut along the lines to make the two sides measuring 36 x 16 inches at one short end and 36 x 10 inches at the other.

3 Measure a point 2 inches from the 16-inch-wide base of both side pieces and use the carpenter's square and the straightedge to draw a line across the width each piece. Fit the top piece of the rack inside and flush with the 10-inch end of both side pieces using the wood screws. Predrill the screw holes before assembling the rack to prevent the wood from splitting. Fit the base piece with the half-drilled holes for the tools facing up inside the 16-inch ends of the side pieces at the line drawn 2 inches up from the base so that the base will be raised 2 inches off the ground when the rack is placed in position.

To reinforce the structure, screw the 1 x 6 x 43-inch rear piece inside the back of the tool rack so that it fits under the top piece. Tighten all the screws to stabilize the rack. Place the rack on a flat surface, and it's ready to use.

We can't resist interesting old tools and reclaimed lumber. From construction dumpsters to garage sales, we've found superb lengths of carved antique elm that now form the head- and footboards of a four-poster bed, massive molded cornices that when stripped of layers of white paint revealed solid oak, and large amounts of both painted and unpainted softwood that we've used for many projects. We have a storage room stacked from floor to ceiling with reclaimed lumber, and some of it was used to build this tool rack.

Garden tool storage is a constant problem at our house. Our accumulation of old and modern tools and garden equipment takes up much of the already-limited space we have, and although we've fitted our tool shed wall with a peg board from which to hang many of the tools, some inevitably end up stacked in a corner of the room. To store some of our straight-handled tools, we decided to construct a simple free-standing rack. You can build this modestly sized rack following our design, or you can adjust it larger or smaller to suit your needs.

# TRELLIS WALL RACK

## EQUIPMENT

Level
Pencil
Hand saw
Electric drill
Wood drill bit (to fit screws)
Awl
Masonry bit (for solid walls)
Screwdriver

## MATERIALS

Old trellis
Two lengths of waste 1 x 1-inch lumber
   (battens)
Selection of wall plugs (for solid walls)
Selection of screws
Metal cup hooks

## METHOD

1 Place the trellis against the wall in the desired position with the horizontal bars facing out, and check that it is level. Mark the wall at the second bar from the top and the second bar from the bottom. Using the hand saw, cut two lengths of the 1 x 1-inch lumber the width of the trellis. Using the electric drill and the wood bit, drill holes in the 1 x 1-inch lumber pieces approximately 8 inches from each end. Align one piece (the top batten) with the marks on the wall and mark the position of the holes in the batten on the wall using the awl. Repeat for the bottom batten. Drill holes into the wall with the electric drill and the masonry bit, fill the holes with the wall plugs, and screw the battens to the wall.

2 Using the wood bit, drill holes through the two thicknesses of the trellis where the vertical bars cross the second horizontal bar from the top and bottom. Place the trellis against the wall so that the battens are hidden by the horizontal bars of the trellis. Secure the trellis in place with screws driven through the holes in the trellis and into the battens on the wall behind, using the level to check for accuracy. Screw the metal cup hooks to the horizontal bars of the trellis as desired.

As our garden evolves, we're often left with old, unused trelliswork. Some we cut down and use in a different location, but when we decided to refurnish our garden room, we reserved one piece to use as a wall storage rack on which to keep all those notes, packets of seeds, and other items that otherwise end up as clutter.

Although this is a very simple project, a trellis rack can be an invaluable addition to a work area or potting shed. We've also attached      rellis pieces to the ceiling of our tool storage area. Using metal S hooks, we can use the trellis to hang garden umbrellas over the winter, terra-cotta wall pots to protect them from the frost, bags of bulbs awaiting planting, and even bunches of flowers to dry.

Although garden trelliswork is easily available and inexpensive, we don't like the colors of commercially stained trelliswork. We prefer to make most of our own from softwood scraps and protect it with exterior-grade wood preservative stained with various pigments to achieve a subdued shade that blends with the col     e wall on which the trellis will be hung.

Before disposing of household or garden relics that appear to be past their useful life, consider how you can reuse them.

Over the past 25 years, we've greatly increased our green wine bottles were stacked in neatly arranged rows from floor to ceiling in the alcove of a high, old stone wall. With the sunlight bouncing off the bases of the bottles, this exciting creation

## INVENTIVE IDEAS

consumption of wine, which means the task of recycling our empty wine bottles is done with a sense of duty rather than youthful enthusiasm. After the last drop of Chardonnay is downed, the empty container is taken out the back door and gets slung into the recycling bin.

We visited a lovely garden where empty green glass wine bottles were saved and used to create an outdoor sculpture. The resembled a huge honeycomb.

Empty wine bottles also can be used to create unique garden attractions—their necks wedged randomly into the stump of a decaying oak tree. Colorful recycled glass chips, which can be purchased at local garden supply stores or salvage dealers, can be used to great effect to create paths, to make mulch, or to add a bit of whimsy to a water garden design.

### RIGHT

A mirror, framed by a mosaic of pebbles, stones, and broken colored china in garden designer Sue Berger's urban garden, leads the visitor toward an imaginary doorway into another secret garden.

### BELOW LEFT

This old oak gate post, complete with its original iron latch, was left in the garden of a village house to create a primitive atmosphere.

### OPPOSITE LEFT

This scarecrow was constructed mainly of old clay flowerpots. With his head of flowering chives, he adds a lighthearted flight of fancy to the garden of a retreat and conference center.

### BELOW RIGHT

Empty wine bottles stacked from floor to ceiling in a garden wall alcove make an eye-catching attraction when illuminated by the sun.

### OPPOSITE CENTER

Weathered coping stones laid in a broken line and overgrown with a profusion of plants in a wildflower bed give the appearance of a fallen and half-buried stone column.

### OPPOSITE RIGHT

This galvanized steel bird feeder was made from a variety of rescued components by a salvage enthusiast who spends much of his leisure time scavenging for the raw materials for his imaginative creations.

Another garden we visited was stuffed with practical and inventive recycling ideas. It sported wine corks on spikes supporting fruit netting without causing damage to the net or harm to the gardener; telephone wires attached to walls for training roses and other climbers; large terra-cotta pots turned upside down and topped with wooden slats to form a work surface; and even a horse's saddle rest attached to an outside wall to hold a garden hose. (The hose holder on page 108 was made from an abandoned electric cable spool.) An old window frame, complete with glass, was put to good use as the lid for a cold frame, and generous-size garden markers were cut from salvaged lumber and roofing slate.

On an agricultural note, old farm equipment can be put to good use in gardens. Stable hay feeders make great planters for colorful flower displays, and old harrows can be fixed to a wall and used as supports for climbing plants. A retired farmer used wooden slats from an unused calf pen and salvaged telephone poles to make a poolside bench and table, while the cart shafts featured on page 118 were decoratively installed to highlight a garden view. Even the peeling white painted wall inside a shed was cleverly adorned with a collection of salvaged artifacts, including rusty tools, a battered wooden shelf, assorted implements, ancient horseshoes, and a skull with antlers!

Less unusual, but equally attractive, are old gutters that can be attached to a wall and planted with summer blooms. Likewise, old clay roof hip tiles and flowerpots attached to ridge tiles and filled with colorful flowers provide a vibrant display from spring through autumn. A simple oak whiskey barrel cut in half and planted with herbs or flowers is another sight seen almost everywhere.

The average garden may not have room for a gargantuan fallen stone "column," cleverly made from salvaged coping stones to create an informal moss-covered border lying strewn on the earth like some prehistoric reptile. We came across just this at a conference center and retreat run by an order of nuns. In the same garden, we turned a corner and to our surprise encountered the figure of a man, made entirely out of old flowerpots, sitting with hoe in hand and chives for hair—a bit of lighthearted fun to frighten off the birds!

Mirrors used on a garden wall are a clever trick that you can use to make a space seem larger, which is particularly useful in small urban gardens. An artist friend attached a bamboo-framed mirror, painted soft lavender blue, to a patio wall and allowed ivy and other creepers to spread and drape themselves around it. They blended so well with the frame that the mirror, at first glance, was disguised, creating the illusion of light in an enlarged area. Garden designer Sue Berger created a handsome Gothic arch from stones, pebbles, shells, and broken china on the ivy-clad wall of her metropolitan garden, fooling the visitor into believing that it leads to another secret enclosure. She also welded together old steel reinforcement rods used to support concrete-wall buildings to form a rusty pergola that in the height of summer is covered in roses, clematis, and a rampant golden leaf vine.

# HOSE HOLDER

## EQUIPMENT

Hand saw
Screwdriver
Jigsaw
Orbital sander or sandpaper
Paintbrush

## MATERIALS

Empty plywood cable spool
Selection of tongue-and-groove wood
    paneling
Selection of ³/₄-inch wood screws
Multipurpose outdoor paint
Four 2¹/₂-inch wood screws

A garden hose is essential in any well-managed garden, but storing it can be a nightmare. Hoses seem to have a life of their own. Wound up in a coil, they always seem to develop tangles; when unwound, the flow of water is prevented by mysteriously appearing kinks and bends. To prolong the life of a hose and to prevent accidental damage, the hose should always be wound on a holder when not in use. Hose holders are available at hardware stores and garden centers, and most do a good job—but at a cost. Here, we show how an effective wall-mounted hose holder can be simply constructed from a discarded cable spool with only basic tools and a little patience.

Cable spools come in many sizes, from gigantic wooden spools mounted on the backs of cable-laying trucks to cardboard spools on which domestic electric cable is sold. Most larger spools are returned to the cable manufacturer for reuse, but if you can get your hands on one, you can transform it into a practical garden table. For this project, we used a plywood electric-cable spool that we found abandoned at an industrial building site, which was the source for many other useful finds.

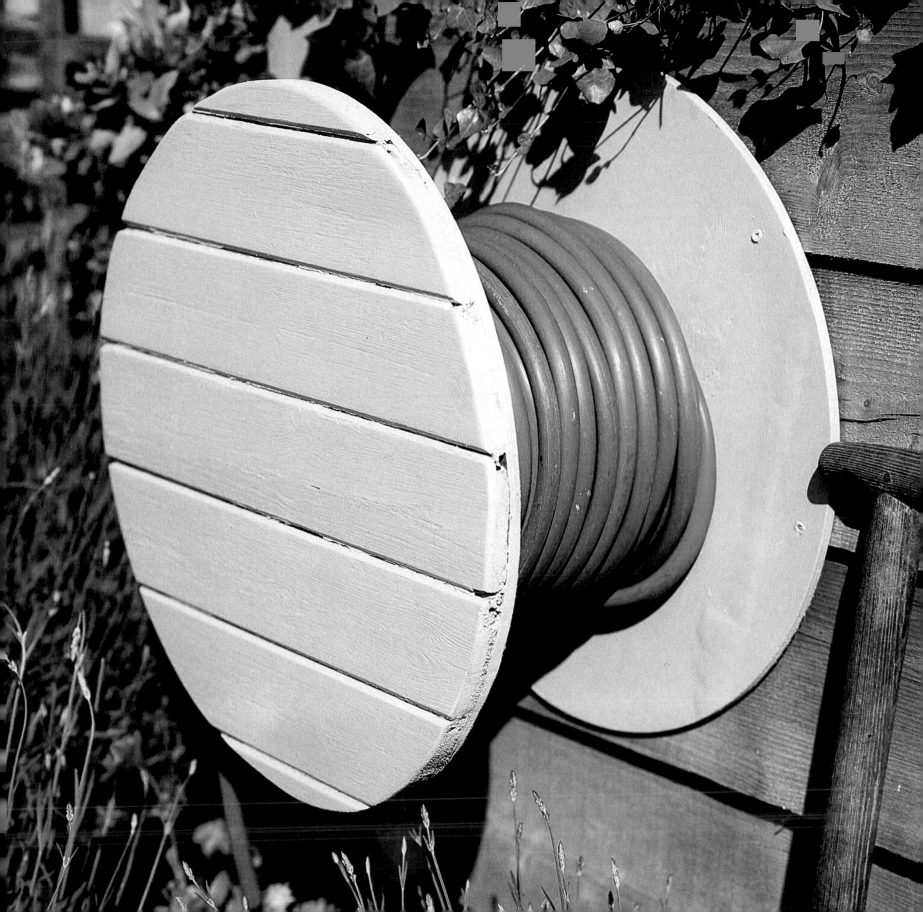

# HOSE HOLDER

## METHOD

1 Saw the tongue-and-groove wood paneling into lengths roughly the diameter of the cable spool, join the boards together, and lay them face down on the work surface. Lay the spool on top of the paneling and screw it to the paneling using two 3/4-inch wood screws to fasten each board.

2 Place the spool with the paneling side down onto a block of wood raised above the work surface and cut the paneling to shape with the jigsaw, using the circular spool base as a guide.

3 Turn the spool over and use the orbital sander or sandpaper to smooth and round the newly cut edge.

4 Apply at least two coats of multipurpose outdoor paint to the entire hose holder, remembering to paint the back side to protect it from water and decay.

5 When the paint is dry, secure the hose holder in position with the four 2$^1$/$_2$-inch wood screws driven through the base of the reel and into the wall behind it. (If the reel is secured to a solid wall, the screws should be driven into wall plugs inserted into previously made holes drilled with a masonry bit.) Touch up exposed screw heads with a dab of the paint. The reel is now ready to use.

# CLAY PIPE PLANTERS

## EQUIPMENT

Garden spade
Garden trowel

## MATERIALS

Selection of clay drainage pipes
Quantity of broken stone or pot shards
Screened soil, compost, or growing medium
Plants
Water
Mulch (optional)

## METHOD

1 Decide where the pipes are to be placed and use the garden spade and trowel to dig a trench slightly deeper than the depth at which you plan to sink the deepest pipe. Place a layer of stone or broken pot shards in the base of the trench to provide a firm footing for the pipes.

2 Place the deepest pipe into position in the trench and then add the other pipes, supporting their bases by building up the foundation of stone and broken pots underneath them. Fill around the base of each pipe with soil, firming the soil around the pipe to secure it in position.

3 Fill the pipes with the screened soil, compost, or growing medium, leaving a bit of space between the soil and the top of the pipes to make watering easier. Add plants to the pipes and water them thoroughly. It can be difficult to control the growth of weeds around grouped pipe planters, so you may want to mulch around their bases.

Terra-cotta drainage pipes are readily available and can be found in numerous lengths, gauges, and finishes. Some are now being replaced with plastic piping, but the traditional clay pipe is still widely used.

Many clay pipes either broken in transit or damaged during installation are a familiar sight around most building developments. Broken pipes are of little or no use to the builder or contractor, and they can often be rescued before they are broken up for fill, their otherwise inevitable end.

Clay pipes can be used to construct effective garden ornamentation. Pipes inserted into the ground at different depths—or a combination of pipes of varying lengths—add height, texture, and an almost architectural quality to a garden, border, or bed. The fact that most pipes are made with one flush and one flanged end offers further opportunities to vary the appearance of the arrangement.

Short lengths of pipe can be very attractive when used as containers inserted into the soil to control the otherwise rampant growth of invasive plants. They also can be attractive when installed flush with the surface of paved areas and filled with low-growing herbs or sweet-smelling plants.

# GARDEN MARKERS

Bunches of twigs and sticks topped with tattered seed packets placed in the garden to identify rows of seedlings or emerging plants can be an eyesore.

Slugs attack most of the packets, the writing on them fades and becomes illegible, and half go missing or are blown or washed away. Plastic markers do an excellent job and can be used to record species and planting dates, but the gardener with an eye to combining practicality and aesthetics will always find a use for attractive and sturdy garden markers that can be easily read and used time and time again.

Slate is an excellent material for making garden markers. It's strong and almost impervious to decay or degradation, and its color and surface are perfect for writing on with chalk or white paint. In "Slate Markers" on page 116, we demonstrate how to transform old roofing slates into simple and long-lasting garden markers.

Wood is another excellent material that can be used to make garden markers, and in "Wood Markers" on page 117 we show how softwood lumber rescued from a broken picket fence can be transformed into unique markers. Almost any type of wood can be used, and if you have access to a circular or table saw, it's simple to cut down waste softwood planks or hardwood lumber to a usable size.

# SLATE MARKERS

## EQUIPMENT

Tape measure
Straightedge
Nail
Slate cutter
Palette knife or paint scraper
Electric orbital sander
   (or various grades of sandpaper
   and emery paper)
Soft cotton rag
Paintbrush

## MATERIALS

Selection of roofing slates
Matte or satin finish
   exterior-grade varnish

## METHOD

All slate has a grain, and roofing slates are generally cut with the grain running along the length of the slate. A slate cutter will make a clean cut across the grain. In this project, we cut the slates into strips along the lengthwise grain.

1 Use the tape measure, the straightedge, and the nail to divide and mark the slates into strips approximately 2¼ inches wide. Cut the strips with the slate cutter. The action of the slate cutter will produce one beveled edge and one flat edge, so always cut the slate with the same face up in order to produce a matching cut on each piece.

2 Cut each strip of slate to the desired length and create a point at one end by cutting from both edges at an angle of approximately 45 degrees. This can be quite tricky and you may break a few points before you master the technique. (Keep the pieces of broken and chipped slate to use as mulch.)

3 Lay the completed markers on a flat surface and remove any flaking material with the palette knife or paint scraper. Use the orbital sander (or varying grades of sandpaper and emery paper) to sand the markers to a smooth finish.

4 Using the soft cotton rag, wipe any dust and debris from the markers and then apply two coats of the matte or satin finish exterior-grade varnish with the paintbrush, letting them dry between coats. When the second coat of varnish is completely dry, the slate garden markers are ready to use.

# WOOD MARKERS

**EQUIPMENT**

Hand saw or miter saw
Paintbrush
Pencil or marker

**MATERIALS**

Lengths of approx. $1/2$ x $2^1/_2$-inch sawn
softwood lumber
White or light-color multipurpose
garden paint

**METHOD**

1 Cut the strips of $1/2$ x $2^1/_2$-inch sawn
softwood timber into approximately 12-inch
lengths. Cut one end to a point using the hand
saw or miter saw.

2 Apply at least two coats of the multipurpose
garden paint to all faces of the strips, paying
particular attention to the point and end grain.
When dry, use the pencil or marker to write on
the markers. Next year, it will be easy to renew
the finish with another coat of paint.

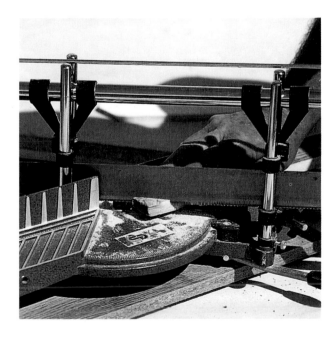

# CART SHAFT ARCHES

**EQUIPMENT**

Paintbrush
Hammer
Sledgehammer
Level
Wrench

**MATERIALS**

Selection of cart shafts
Exterior-grade transparent wood
    preservative
Scrap wood for supports
Selection of nails
2 metal fence spikes per shaft
Scrap block of wood to fit
    inside metal spikes
Selection of wooden wedges

We bought the cart shafts used for this project at an auction. Included in the lot were a selection of harnesses, some old brass pieces, and a number of mysterious iron and wooden objects, the purposes of which we only discovered later from a farmer who had spent his early life working horses.

Made obsolete by modern farming methods, early working horse harnesses and tools are now rusting and rotting away on country farms—a fast-disappearing resource for functional artifacts largely ignored by collectors and museums. We used some of the metal pieces and harnesses as decorations but ignored the heavy shafts for many months.

When a herd of cattle almost destroyed our yard, the only answer was to rototill the entire lawn and lay new sod. Three months later, we had a new lawn that stretched down to our small orchard and the open countryside beyond. We wanted to emphasize that view and decided to erect three of the shafts to frame the longest vista. We used another shaft as an archway leading to a garden seating area, and we have plans to erect more as *objets d'art*.

# CART SHAFT ARCHES

**METHOD**

1 Before you begin constructing the arches, saturate the cart shafts with the exterior-grade transparent wood preservative to treat any rot and to protect the wood from further decay. Pay particular attention to the end grain and any wood that will be below the ground.

2 Nail a piece of the scrap wood to each shaft to form temporary supports. Erect the cart shafts in the garden, moving them around until you find the best position for each shaft. Stand back and view them from a distance and then fine-tune their positions until you have achieved the effect you want.

3 Lay the shafts on the ground just behind their proposed positions and remove the temporary supports. For each shaft, use the sledgehammer cushioned by a block of wood to drive a metal fence spike for each upright into the ground. Start by driving the spike halfway, check with the level that it is upright, and then continue to drive the spike into the ground until only its socket is visible, making sure the tightening bolt is still accessible.

4 You will need help with the final step of this project. Place the uprights of each cart shaft into the metal spikes and, while someone holds the shaft vertical, anchor the uprights in the spikes using the wooden wedges. Use the level to check that each shaft is vertical and then tighten the integral bolt on each spike with the wrench to ensure that each shaft is secure.

# LOG BIRD FEEDER

## EQUIPMENT

Electric drill and 1¼-inch hole cutter bit
1-inch wood chisel

## MATERIALS

Wooden log
Empty metal tea light candle holders
Three 1½-inch galvanized screw eyes
Lightweight chain
Three small key rings or snap hooks
Large key ring or snap hook
Melted fat
Chopped peanuts or bird seed

## METHOD

An old, lightweight log was selected for this project to make a feeder that would be large enough to hold a reasonable quantity of bird food but light enough to hang from a slender branch, which would discourage visits from larger birds.

1 Place the log on a flat surface and, using the electric drill and hole cutter bit, drill several recesses in the top surface of the log to a depth of approximately 1½ inches.

2 Using the chisel, remove the cores of cut wood from the drilled recesses and scrape the bases level.

3 Screw the three galvanized screw eyes into the ends of the log to provide secure anchorage points for the hanging chain. Cut the lightweight chain (salvaged, if possible) into three equal lengths. Join one end of each piece of chain to each of the screw eyes using a small key ring or snap hook, and then join the remaining ends of the chain together with the large key ring or snap hook.

4 Place an empty tea light candle holder into each drilled hole in the top surface of the log and fill them with a mixture of melted fat and chopped peanuts or bird seed. Let the fat cool. Hang the bird feeder from an outer branch of a tree for the wild birds to discover and enjoy. Keep a few empty tea lights filled with the fat and seed mixture, and when the first containers are empty, replace them.

Everyone welcomes birds and wildlife into their gardens. Kitchen scraps, wild bird seed, a hanging coconut, and string bags full of peanuts all provide vital food for birds (and the occasional squirrel) during the winter. Large numbers of the wild bird population die over the winter, and garden birds can come to depend on the food put out for them. If you care for wildlife, it's a good idea to provide clean food and fresh water year-round. A regular supply of food can mean survival, particularly to fledgling birds in spring.

We enjoy watching the bird life that surrounds our home. Three species of swans gather over the winter on the fields beyond our garden, wild ducks abound, and the cries of curlew are constant. Both green and larger spotted woodpeckers are common, and we keep a patch of garden wild to attract goldfinches. Recently we've seen an increasing number of hawks, but the most destructive of all our visiting birds are the myriad noisy, bullying magpies that have proliferated over recent years.

With no shortage of tree branches, we decided to construct a simple hanging bird feeder that would attract a cross-section of the smaller species but thwart the plundering of gray squirrels and the larger crows and magpies that otherwise steal the food.

# WINDOW COLD FRAME

## EQUIPMENT

Orbital sander or sandpaper
    and sanding block
Tape measure
Hand saw
Electric drill and wood drill bit
Electric screwdriver bit
Pencil or marker
Straightedge
Jigsaw or hand saw
Electric planer
Paintbrush

## MATERIALS

Old window frame
Quantity of softwood planks approx.
    1 x 6 inches
Quantity of softwood approx.
    2 x 2 inches
Quantity of 2½-inch galvanized screws
Quantity of softwood approx.
    1 x 2 inches
Length of softwood approx.
    1 x 2 x 10 inches
Two metal washers
White or light-color opaque or multipurpose
    garden paint

In the absence of a greenhouse, no garden should be without a coldframe, a place where plants can be started early and where they will be protected from the cold and frost. Avid organic gardeners enjoy home-grown vegetables, safe in the knowledge that they've been fed only well-cured garden compost and are free of pesticides and sprays. Somehow the vegetables taste so much better.

Unfortunately, the growing season in many areas is all too short. In past years, we've protected our newly sown plants with glass cloches rescued from a local strawberry grower who was replacing them with plastic tunnels. The problem with cloches is that they break easily, are heavy, and are difficult to store when not in use. Luckily we had the materials handy to make a number of cold frames to replace them. For the tops, we used old windows with frames and glass intact, bought at a local warehouse sale. For the frames, we decided to use some softwood planks, once used to line a roof and rescued from a local reclamation yard just for the cost of collecting them.

Discarded windows are easy to find and should be inexpensive. They make a wonderful resource and can be used as doors for wall cupboards in a kitchen, made into coffee tables, and even reused as windows in garden sheds and garages.

# WINDOW COLD FRAME

## METHOD

When selecting a window frame for this project, check that the putty securing the glass in place is sound and that there are no gaps or holes that will allow moisture to penetrate the wood and encourage rot. We selected a number of window frames of equal size to make several matching cold frames.

1 Use the orbital sander or the sandpaper and sanding block to remove any residual paint from the window frame. If the paint is in relatively good condition, sand it to a smooth surface.

2 Measure the width of the 1 x 6-inch softwood planks you will be using for the project and decide on the height of the proposed cold frame. Since the cold frame is designed to slope from back to front, we used three planks for the back and two for the front. Cut two lengths of the 2 x 2-inch softwood approximately 1 inch less than the combined width of two of the 1 x 6-inch planks. Cut two lengths approximately 1 inch less than the combined width of three of the 1 x 6-inch planks. This will give you two short and two long battens. Cut six lengths of the 1 x 6-inch planking approximately 2 inches longer than the shorter side of the window frame to form the sides of the cold frame. Place three of the six planks on a work surface and join them together with a short batten at one end and a long batten at the other, predrilling the screw holes where they fall close to the ends of the planks in order to prevent the wood from splitting. Repeat with the remaining three planks and two battens to form the second side piece, ensuring that when placed together the corresponding battens face each other.

3 Cut five lengths from the 1 x 6-inch planking, each approximately 2 inches longer than the longer side of the window frame, to form the front and back of the cold frame. Place three planks together on a work surface and measure their combined width. These three pieces will form the back of the frame. Measure the combined width of the remaining two planks, which will form the front of the frame. Take one of the assembled side pieces and mark a point at each end, the first at the height of the front of the frame and the second on the opposite end at a point approximately 1/2 inch less than the height of the back of the frame. Use the pencil or marker and straightedge to draw a line from the first point to the second point and cut the side piece to shape along the marked line using the jigsaw or hand saw. Repeat with the second side piece.

4 Take the two planks cut for the frame front and predrill two holes at both ends of each plank approximately 1 inch from the end, one close to the top and one close to the bottom. Fit the two planks to the sloping side pieces to form the front of the frame, screwing through the predrilled holes into the battens. Repeat with the three remaining planks to form the rear of the frame. The cold frame base is now assembled.

5 Place the assembled base on a level work surface and use the electric planer to plane the tops of the front and back of the frame level with the slope of the side pieces. Always plane away from the ends toward the center of the wood to minimize the risk of the planer snagging on and damaging the side pieces. To form a frame to hold the window on top of the base, cut the 1 x 2-inch softwood into four pieces with the inner edge of each piece just larger than the rebate size of the window and the outside edge overlapping the sides of the base. Predrill and attach each piece of the frame in place with screws driven into the top of the base. Place the window into the rebate to check the fit. Take the piece of 1 x 2 x 10-inch softwood lumber and drill a screw hole in it at approximately one-third its length. Using the two washers behind the screw, attach the piece of wood at the top of the inside face of the cold frame and at the center of the top plank to form a support that can be used to keep the window open to provide ventilation for growing plants in warmer weather. The washers behind the screw will make it easier to move the support. Finally, paint the completed cold frame with two coats of white or light-color opaque or multipurpose garden paint.

In *Salvage Style for Outdoor
Living,* we've given you hints
and ideas about sources and
different uses for salvaged
materials. We've advised you to
look around yourself, to think

In some areas, local planning
authorities require the use of
historically accurate materials. If
you're working on a building in
such a historic area, you may
be required to use such

# HOW TO GET IT, HOW TO DO IT

before you dispose of anything,
and never to rush into buying
new if there is a reclaimed
material that can be used.

Reclamation yards are the
supermarkets of salvage—where
a bewildering array of wood, tiles,
bricks, and artifacts awaits the
buyer. The days when all
reclaimed materials could be
purchased for less than their
modern counterparts are gone,
but unless you are prepared to
search for these objects yourself,
salvage yards are the solution for
the enthusiast who wants to
enjoy recycled materials.

materials. Remember that when
a building is listed in a historic
register, the land on which it
stands is also listed, so be sure
to seek approval from the proper
authorities before planning
any alterations or doing any
construction work in the house
or garden. In some conservation
areas, even the colors used for
decoration are controlled. There
also are strict rules governing the
cutting and pruning of trees,
particularly if they are the subject
of a preservation order. A tree
takes years to grow, but it can
be cut down in only an hour.

**ABOVE**

A selection of roof ventilators removed from old buildings await buyers in a reclamation yard. One of these verdigris copper ventilators was transformed into an imposing dovecote.

**ABOVE RIGHT**

A stunning floor in a summer house was carefully restored using as much of the original brick and stone as possible.

**OPPOSITE**

An eclectic selection of architectural antiques and miscellaneous salvage is lined up and labeled for sale at an auction held on the grounds of a country house.

Consider local laws and regulations carefully before attempting major work in your garden. If you are in doubt, check with your local planning agency. We owe it to our predecessors, and those who will follow us, not to alter, damage, or destroy something that is fundamentally irreplaceable. Every tree felled to make way for a patio and every window replaced by an unsightly PVC double-glazed unit are more nails in the coffin of the diminishing resource of our historic past.

There is nothing intrinsically wrong with using new materials. Architects and garden designers are responsible for much of the current interest in contemporary design and they use many modern materials, some of which can and do outperform their obsolete predecessors. There is, however, a time and a place for everything, and in *Salvage Style for Outdoor Living,* we hope we've persuaded you to look again at what others have discarded and showed you how challenging and exciting working with old and discarded materials can be.

Visit gardens wherever and whenever you can. Many gardens have used salvaged materials extensively. Many inspirational private gardens are open to the public through local and national garden foundations that raise funds for charity from entrance fees.

Adapt the projects in this book to what you have available. Use different materials and components. Experiment with things you have discovered, some of which perhaps are unique to the part of the world in which you live. And if you have the space, collect and store discovered items that you may not have a immediate use for but are sure you will find a purpose for one day.

## SOURCES OF SALVAGED MATERIALS

Time and again in *Salvage Style for Outdoor Living*, we've suggested you keep your eyes open for that opportune find. Sources of discarded artifacts, lumber, and building materials are all around you, and should you be fortunate to see an opportunity to salvage something, don't overlook it.

Reclamation yards are an invaluable source of salvaged materials. Most dealers specialize, and doing a little research trying to find the expert in the field is time well spent. We are committed supporters of SALVO (see "Sources" on page 138) and its voluntary code of conduct. SALVO code dealers keep a record of the origin of everything they sell. They agree not to buy any item if there is the slightest suspicion that it may be stolen, and

they will not sell anything removed from a historically listed building or monument. The theft of architectural and garden antiques is growing worldwide, and SALVO members have helped the police recover numerous stolen articles.

Most reclamation dealers are experts in their field and are eager to share their knowledge. If they don't know the answer to a question, they will know someone who does. Dealers are extremely busy on weekends, when much of their business is done. Don't bother otherwise helpful dealers if this prevents them from attending to other customers. Instead, return during the week when they are less busy. The yard is more likely to be frequented by trade customers then, and the prices may be lower.

Salvage yards can be a source of materials at bargain prices. Hidden behind the stacks of bricks on pallets, the carefully sorted tiles, or piles of softwood lumber may well be a treasure trove of useful materials, yours for the asking. Dealers have a problem disposing of broken items and scraps. If you can use it, make them an offer. Most of the broken tiles and slates used for edging in "A Garden Reclaimed" (see page 60) were found in a dumpster at a reclamation yard. At another yard, we secured a job lot of roofing lumber that was too full of nails to be economical for the yard to remove. No problem for us, though. We used the lumber to make our Potting Stand in "Seating and Retreating" (see page 24) and the Window Cold Frame in "Inventive Ideas" (see page 124).

Never ignore dealers that handle government surplus. A bewildering array of government and military equipment is sold to dealers who offer the items at often ludicrously cheap prices to the public. Old army ammunition boxes are ideal for storing tools and the odds and ends that clutter up most garden rooms and potting sheds.

The Bucket Planter we made in "Plants, Planters, and Planting" (see page 34) came from a government surplus dealer, and other finds have included old tent poles that were used to construct a garden arbor, the buckets used as planters in "The Themed Garden" (see page 80), and numerous tools we've put to good use in our own garden. Most things made for the armed forces were manufactured to exacting standards, and many are ideally suited for reuse in the home or garden.

If you haven't yet visited salvage yards that carry government surplus, do so. They provide a fascinating insight into government

**BELOW**

Looking through a cart shaft into a reclamation yard, where a mouthwatering assortment of rural artifacts, bric-a-brac, salvage, and antiques are offered for sale at sometimes remarkably low prices.

wastefulness and are a valuable resource for the enthusiastic salvager.

Scan the classified ads in your local newspapers for bargains. Many newspapers run free ads for articles less than a certain value—a worthwhile way of disposing of unwanted items. The advertiser may not want the item, but it could be quite valuable to you.

We've secured numerous items from newspaper classified ads. Lumber rescued from an old greenhouse—now incorporated in a garden shelter—was one of our best finds. The wooden fencing that protects part of our garden was made from parts of a demolished building that we found advertised, and even the chickens we keep in our garden are the descendants of some hens we bought as the result of a small classified ad.

Flea markets are a godsend to the keen-eyed salvager. While they've achieved something of a reputation as an outlet for the disposal of goods with a questionable history, flea markets are where unwanted home and garden items can be bought at bargain prices. Many of the plants and shrubs in our garden and the old glass garden lights and paraffin lamps we use for outdoor dining were bought at flea markets.

Garage sales also can be rewarding. At one of the most recent we attended, the owners were leaving the country and were disposing of a lifetime's accumulation of home and garden tools and equipment. We bought dozens of terra-cotta pots and a collection of neglected but robust garden tools, now invaluably employed in our garden.

Scan the newspaper for details of farm sales and auctions. Farm sales can be busy social occasions where sales of livestock and equipment accumulated over generations of farming life take second place to meeting around the mobile catering van to discuss the woes of modern farming. The water trough used for the Water Garden in "The Themed

Garden" (see page 76) and the cheese presses for the Cheese Press Table in "Seating and Retreating" (see page 18) were found at farm sales. If you live in a rural area, farm sales can be rewarding and enjoyable hunting grounds for old, unused treasures.

Architectural and garden antique and salvage sales are increasing in popularity. Many artifacts fetch staggering prices at these sales, but you can still find bargains. We bought the cart and carriage shafts used in "Inventive Ideas" (see page 118) at such an auction, and one of our most satisfying purchases—a wonderful resource of hardwood lumber and moldings—was made at a recent sale.

Never ignore builders' dumpsters. A search through a roadside dumpster can reveal a cornucopia of useful things. The scaffold boards used to construct the Scaffold Bench in "Seating and Retreating" (see page 14) were salvaged from a dumpster. (To avoid being accused of theft, always get permission from the homeowner or builder before removing anything from a dumpster.)

You may find a building that is being demolished where the lumber will be burned, the bricks sent to a landfill, and the roofing slates discarded. Make the contractor an offer for some of the discarded materials, or better still, offer to take them off his hands. Disposing of unwanted materials is expensive, and the value of some salvaged building materials is outweighed by the cost of sorting them. If you see something useful, approach the contractor. If you don't get in the way or hold up the work, you may be able to walk away with some wonderful raw materials.

We frequently stumble upon building sites where valuable materials are being thrown away. On a recent shopping trip, we discovered a department store that was being gutted to make way for a new housing development. Shop fixtures were being

discarded, paneling destroyed, and hundreds of bricks had been thrown into a dumpster. After a brief chat with the site foreman, we left with the back of the car filled with bricks. After spending only an hour cleaning them, we had more than enough clean bricks to construct the edging used for the raised garden in "A Garden Reclaimed" (see page 50).

Housing development sites are another wonderful source of salvageable materials. You'll be surprised by the number of old pipes that are abandoned on site, too damaged to be used by the builder but fine for the Pipe Planter in "Inventive Ideas" (see page 112). Lumber scraps from roof trusses and floor joists, broken roof tiles, and bricks abound—if you don't save them, they will be burned or end up as rubble or landfill. Construction sites are dangerous, and access to most of them is restricted. Never venture onto a site without permission, and always seek permission before removing anything from the site.

Scrap-metal yards contain a wealth of useful items. We've salvaged copper pipes to make a greenhouse sprinkler system, used scrap lead sheeting to protect the tops of fencing posts and to protect an outdoor building, and even adapted discarded steel reinforcing bars to construct a light and airy garden pergola. Scrap yards can also be dangerous places. Let the owner know what you are looking for and he will help you. Your finds will be weighed, and you should be asked for little more than their scrap value.

Auto salvage yards can be a source of inspiration. We've seen wonderful planters constructed from old hubcaps and were enchanted by the centerpiece of the garden of a Citroën enthusiast—an old model 2CV overflowing with flowering plants.

The World Wide Web is a growing source of salvaged and recycled materials and information. Internet Web sites that we've found useful are www.salvoweb.com, which lists reclamation and salvage dealers worldwide and provides links to numerous other sites; www.recycle.net, which runs Recycler's World and a materials buying and selling Web site; and www.arcsal.com, a simple-to-use and well-illustrated Web directory of salvage, reclaimed materials, and architectural and garden antiques.

Finally, look around your own home and think first before you throw something away. Many useful items can be reincarnated in another form. Old buckets that might appear to be past their usefulness can be transformed into striking garden planters. If they are too deteriorated, sink them into the soil to contain invasive plants. Corrugated metal can be cut down with metal shears to make lawn edging, and even that old and broken chair can become a planter, overflowing with scented chamomile. Often we find ourselves searching through dumpsters and reclamation yards to replace an item we once had but threw away. The Trellis Wall Rack in "Elements and Ambiance" (see page 102) is an example of how we put to a different use something that could have been discarded.

# HINTS AND TECHNIQUES

## SAFETY FIRST

Safety is very important. Before you start any project or building activity, be sure you have the correct tools and that they are all in working order. Take every precaution to prevent unnecessary accidents. Damaged tools are dangerous, and faulty power tools are deadly. Check your power tools for any damage and have them regularly maintained. Think through each project before you start following the directions, and clear the work area of any extraneous materials or equipment.

If you're using sharp equipment such as chisels or power saws, always cut away from yourself. A moment's inattention can result in a nasty wound. Never cut close to your hand; securely clamp the item you're cutting to a work surface, and use a scrap of wood to push lumber through a planer or table saw. Think first, cut second.

Most importantly, keep all tools, equipment and substances that are likely to be dangerous out of the reach of children and animals.

## TOXIC SUBSTANCES

Many projects involve the use of preservatives, stains, and other potentially dangerous substances. Read and follow the instructions on the container and make sure you have rags on hand to clean up spilled materials. Never casually dispose of any waste or empty containers that may pollute the environment or react with other discarded substances.

In the past, wood was painted with lead-based paints. This material is hazardous, and you must wear a dust mask if you are sanding or planing down old paint. Dust from any substance can be dangerous, and if you are working without a dust vacuum system, a dust mask or full face mask is essential.

The dangers of asbestos are well known. Asbestos can be present in old buildings that are being demolished or renovated. Strict laws govern its removal, and only registered experts, properly equipped, are allowed to do this work. Occasionally, traces of asbestos can be found on wood that has been salvaged from old buildings. Some amateurs undertaking home improvements fail to recognize asbestos and unknowingly deposit it in a roadside dumpster. Always err on the side of caution. If in doubt, leave it alone.

## PROTECTIVE CLOTHING

Wear the correct clothing for the job. Loose clothing can become entangled in moving parts of power equipment, and injuries can be caused by careless operation. Always work with your sleeves buttoned. Ties or scarves can be extremely dangerous, and long hair should be tied up or covered.

Proper protective clothing is essential. A face or dust mask, protective gloves, and coveralls should be part of your workshop inventory. Eye protection is extremely important when using any power equipment. We own a full face mask that is attached as a visor to a protective helmet. Obtained from Tools Direct (see "Sources" on page 138), a company that helped us with this book, the visor is comfortable to use and ideal when operating a chain or power saw.

Protective clothing is essential if you're using a chain saw and advisable if you're working with sheet metal. Hard hats are legally required at most building and demolition sites, and you should never be without one if you plan to venture onto such a site. Steel-toe safety shoes or boots with protective soles are a good investment, as well as a strong pair of leather gloves.

## ELECTRICITY OUTDOORS

Electricity is dangerous, and the combination of electricity and water can be lethal. Never use electrical equipment outdoors if it is raining, and always keep wires and plugs out of wet areas. If any electrical wires become damaged, replace them rather than attempt to repair them.

Some electrical fittings are specifically manufactured for outdoor use, and unless you

**TOP**

Stable bricks are made in a wide range of patterns, and these examples were found in a reclamation yard.

**BOTTOM**

A weathered and worn oak sherry barrel, complete with its original stencil marking, sits among a stack of wooden pallets.

are experienced, these should be installed by a qualified electrician. Have all outdoor electrical installations checked by a qualified electrician before use.

Water gardens are increasing in popularity, and many involve a pump or other electrical equipment. Seek the advice of an expert water garden retailer before you install such equipment. OASE (see "Sources" on page 138), a manufacturer of pumps and water garden equipment, has a helpful Web site that is very informative.

## FIRST AID

Work involving sharp tools or power equipment can be dangerous, and a basic first-aid kit should be kept handy in case of accidents. Familiarize yourself with its contents and always keep it well stocked.

## EQUIPMENT AND TOOLS

Most projects in *Salvage Style for Outdoor Living* require only simple tools. Black and Decker (see "Sources" on page 138) provided us with some very useful power tools to prepare the projects for this book, and you'll find many of these tools extremely helpful. A well-equipped workshop should include a number of basic tools. Remember, the better the quality of tool you purchase, the better it will perform and the longer it will last.

Keep your tools in good condition and store them properly. Metal tools, which might be affected by moisture, should be protected with a wipe or spray of oil when not in use. As much as possible, store tools in a dry environment. Screws, nails, and other supplies should be kept in airtight containers.

We rent tools for many projects—a cement mixer for larger jobs and a diamond-blade saw for slicing bricks and cutting slate. The rental store will also supply the appropriate safety equipment.

## USING OLD LUMBER

Over time, both hardwood and softwood lumber develop a patina and coloration, part of a wood's attractiveness. Salvage old lumber whenever possible, removing any nails or hardware and storing it in a dry area where air can circulate around it. Oak, a particularly attractive hardwood, can be discolored by iron or steel nails or screws. If metal fixings are required, use brass.

Salvaged wood can be used for many garden projects, and examples of now-rare wood can be found in salvage yards and old buildings. It is important to remove nails and hardware before using power equipment, or you may seriously damage your tools.

Painted softwood can be stripped at home using a paint-stripping solution, which is time-consuming, or you can take the wood to a commercial paint-stripping company that will dip the wood into a hot caustic solution. This process can loosen joints and cause some discoloration, so don't strip hardwood in a caustic solution. Old paint can be removed by sanding with a machine or by hand. You can also use a heat gun, but be very careful not to scorch the underlying wood.

Always treat reclaimed lumber with a wood preservative to prevent deterioration. A number of colored and colorless wood preservatives are available, and Cuprinol (see "Sources" on page 138), which helped us with this book, also produces an effective wood hardener that can be used if the wood has started to deteriorate. Lumber that will be in contact with the ground or underground should be saturated with a preservative before use. Place the wood in a container holding the preservative and let it soak overnight to saturate. If you're using new wood in these situations, make sure it is a rot-resistant wood such as cedar.

## BRICKS, TILES, AND TERRA-COTTA

Old bricks, tiles, and terra-cotta were produced in small factories in an extraordinary variety of shapes and colors. Manufactured from local clay and distributed only within a small area, these materials range in color from pale cream to almost black. Although in later years they were made to an almost-standard size, bricks can be found glazed, unglazed, perforated, high-fired for use in factories, or even patterned for stable use. Many bear the mark of their maker—testimony to a once-thriving local industry.

Handmade bricks were produced by throwing wet clay into wooden molds before air drying and firing. Some handmade bricks still bear the fingerprints of their long-dead makers. When sliced in half (rent a diamond-blade saw to do this), old bricks reveal stunning patterns of swirling colors. Sealed with linseed oil or tile sealant, old bricks make very attractive flooring. Roofing tiles were produced to individual local designs, and your local reclamation yard should have a selection of indigenous patterns.

You will have to clean the mortar from most old bricks, and this can be a time-consuming job requiring a bricklayer's trowel or brick or masonry bolster. Stained bricks can be cleaned with a commercial brick cleaner, which can be a smelly and unpleasant job. Bricks can be used in their original condition for paths and edging, but some types are susceptible to water penetration and frost damage. Use engineering-grade bricks if your project will be exposed to severe weather conditions.

Roofing tiles make excellent pavers for patios and are also good for capping walls. In "Seating and Retreating" on page 11, we used roofing tiles for the floor in a seating area, and in "Inventive Ideas" on page 105, we used clay tiles to edge a garden path. Broken tiles make very effective garden edging (see "A Garden Reclaimed" on page 47) and can be used as a base underneath concrete or to provide drainage in garden pots and planters.

Damaged terra-cotta pots and urns can be repaired with a two-part epoxy resin glue. A specialized two-part, cold-setting, colored epoxy putty also can be used to repair and fill broken terra-cotta.

## SLATE

Slate is one of the most versatile reclaimed materials that you can use in the garden. We use both whole and broken roofing slates for edging, for practical garden markers or memo boards, and as mulch. Large slates are an ideal paving material and make perfect weatherproof tops for garden tables.

Roofing slates can be cut with a slate cutter or a small water-cooled, diamond-bladed, electrical tile cutter, both of which are available at home improvement stores or rental agencies. Larger pieces of slate should be cut by a professional, although you can rent a specialized rotary saw for this job. Although most old roofing slates have suffered delamination through years of exposure to the elements, we've showed you how to return slate to an almost pristine condition in a number of the projects in *Salvage Style for Outdoor Living*.

## RECLAIMED METALS

Reclaimed metal and metal objects have innumerable uses in the garden. Old buckets make attractive planters, and reinforcing rods and sheets can be used to construct pergolas and arches for climbing plants. Some welding may be required. This is not a job for the amateur, so you may want to hire an experienced welder.

A large variety of salvaged metals can be found at scrap-metal yards. We've found old copper piping for garden irrigation systems and some unique fencing. Thin sheet steel and zinc can be pot-riveted to construct fashionable planters, and scrap sheet lead is extremely useful for waterproofing drainage paths and covering the tops of posts.

Most salvaged metals show evidence of oxidation or corrosion. At best, they will have tarnished or developed a patina through exposure to the elements. Some patination can be attractive, but to prevent further degradation and potential structural damage, salvaged metals should be protected with an appropriate paint or finish. A number of single-coat metal paints are now available, so ask your paint retailer for advice. To preserve the appearance of bright metals, spray them with metal lacquer.

## CEMENT, CONCRETE, AND MORTAR

Cement is the basic component of concrete and mortar, together with sand, gravel, or stone aggregate and, in days gone by, lime or ash. Different mixes are required for different purposes, although you can save time and trouble by using commercially available ready-mixed, general-purpose concrete and bricklaying mortars.

*Sands and aggregates in general use are*

**SHARP SAND** A coarse, gritty material normally used with other aggregates to make concrete.

**SOFT OR BUILDER'S SAND** This has finer particles and is used for bricklaying mortar.

**COARSE AGGREGATE, GRAVEL, OR CRUSHED STONE** Particles normally between 1/4 inch and 3/4 inch in diameter are used to make concrete.

**BALLAST OR AGGREGATE** A mixture of coarse aggregate and sharp sand that is used to make concrete. Normally premixed in the ratio of 2 parts coarse aggregate to 1 part sharp sand.

*For most external construction, the usual mixtures are*

**BRICKLAYING MORTAR** 1 part cement to 4 parts soft sand.

**BLOCKWORK OR STONE MORTAR** 1 part cement to 5 parts soft sand.

**CONCRETE FOR DRIVEWAYS AND HEAVY LOAD AREAS** 1 part cement to 2 parts sharp sand and 4 parts coarse aggregate.

**CONCRETE FOR PATHS AND PATIOS, BASES FOR GARDEN SHEDS AND OTHER LIGHT-LOAD AREAS** 1 part cement to 3 parts sharp sand and 6 parts coarse aggregate.

If concrete is laid to a depth of less than 3 inches, a more durable mixture is required. Concrete foundations and paths require a sub-base of at least 3 inches of broken stone, bricks, or other rubble.

All the measurements are by volume—use a bucket for measuring purposes. Concrete and mortar should be mixed with a shovel on a flat surface (a sheet of scrap plywood is ideal) or in a wheelbarrow (clean thoroughly after use). Mix the dry components, then add the cement, continuing to mix until an even color is achieved. Shape the mixture into a mound, make a hole in the center, and add water slowly, mixing constantly until a consistency is achieved that allows you to use the shovel to make a series of ridges on the surface that hold their shape.

Newly mixed concrete and mortar should be used within 2 hours. It dries quickly but will not achieve its full strength for about 7 days. Cover new concrete work with large plastic sheets to protect it from rain and extremes of heat and cold. In very hot weather, light spraying with water once a day for a week will prevent it from deteriorating. Addition of an accelerator and a frost protector to the mixture will help drying during cold weather.

Various additives were traditionally used with mortar, particularly lime, which made it easier to work and allowed some flexibility in the finished work. Lime mortars are smoother and more durable than their modern counterparts. Seek the advice of an expert restoration contractor when using lime mortars. However, similar results can be achieved by making a mixture of 1 part cement, 1/2 part lime, and 2 to 4 parts soft sand. Modern masonry mortars containing up to one-third limestone filler can be bought, some containing a plasticizer.

Try to match the color of existing mortar by using local sand (or stone dust) whenever possible. Cement coloring additives are available, but they should be used with caution because the mortar will change color when dry and as time passes.

## PAINTS AND STAINS

Add interest and color to garden lumber with paints and stains. We mix our own stains with transparent wood preservative to achieve effective results. Many modern garden paints contain preservatives, and Cuprinol (see "Sources" on page 138) makes products specially formulated for garden use that are both attractive and easy to use. Cuprinol's multipurpose paints provide excellent results on stone, brick, concrete block, wood, and even rubber and metal.

If traditional paints are being used on planed wood surfaces, the lumber should be primed and undercoated before the application of the final paint finish. If the wood is being varnished, use a product designed for outdoor application because interior varnishes will not stand prolonged exposure to weather.

Many paints and stains are now available, so there should be no limit to your garden palette.

# SOURCES

## TOOLS AND SUPPLIES

**BLACK AND DECKER**
Tel: 800-544-6986
Web site:
www.blackanddecker.com
Electric and battery-powered
hand garden tools for the
professional and hobbyist.

**LOWES**
Tel: 800-44LOWES
Web site: www.lowes.com
Screws, nails, hardware and
tools, plumbing and
electrical supplies, lumber.

**SCREWFIX DIRECT**
Tel: 0500 414141
Fax: 0800 0562256
E-mail:
online@screwfix.com
Web site:
www.screwfix.com
Screws, nails, hardware and
tools, plumbing and
electrical supplies.

**THE HOME DEPOT**
Tel: 800-430-3376
Web site:
www.homedepot.com
Screws, nails, hardware and
tools, plumbing and
electrical supplies, lumber.

## PAINTS, STAINS AND WOOD TREATMENT PRODUCTS

**CUPRINOL PRODUCTS**
101 Prospect Avenue
Cleveland, OH 44115
Tel: 800-424-5837
Fax: 800-434-7076
E-mail:
cuprinol@sherwin.com
Web site:
www.cuprinol.com
Wood treatment products,
stains, and color washes for
interior and exterior use.

## INFORMATION ON RECLAMATION AND ARCHITECTURAL ANTIQUES, DEALERS, CRAFTSPEOPLE AND SERVICES

**SALVO**
P.O. Box 333
Cornhill-upon-Tweed
Northumberland, England
TD12 4YJ
Tel: 01890 820333
Fax: 01890 820499
E-mail: tk@salvoweb.com
Web site:
www.salvoweb.com
Publishers of information on
architectural antiques,
reclaimed materials,
reclamation dealers, and
craftspeople working with
salvage. They are the
originators of the SALVO
Code and the SALVO Code
Dealer list. The Web site
links many different dealers
from around the world.

## GARDEN ARCHITECTURAL ANTIQUES, RECLAMATION AND SALVAGE DEALERS

**AARDVARK ANTIQUES**
475 Thames Street
Newport, RI 02840
Tel: 401-849-7233
Fax: 401-849-1591
Architectural antiques,
furniture, fountains, carousel
horses, stained glass.

**ADKINS ARCHITECTURAL ANTIQUES**
3515 Fannin Street
Houston, TX 77004
Tel: 713-522-6547
Fax: 713-529-8253
Architectural antiques,
stained-glass windows,
garden decor, patio furniture,
urns, benches, fountains.

**ADMAC SALVAGE**
111 Saranac Street
Littleton, NH 03561
Tel: 603-444-1200
Web site:
www.musar.com/Admac
Architectural antiques, barn
boards, windows.

**AMERICAN SALVAGE**
7001 NW 27th Avenue
Miami, FL 33147
Tel: 305-691-7001
Fax: 305-691-0001
Architectural salvage and
building supplies.

**AMERICAN TIMBERS LLC**
P.O. Box 430
Canterbury, CT 06331
Tel: 800-461-8660
Fax: 860-546-9334
Recycled lumber.

**ANTIQUE ARTICLES**
P.O. Box 72
North Billerica, MA 01862
Tel/Fax: 978-663-8083
Web site:
www.antiquearticles.com
Antique tiles.

**ARCHITECTURAL ACCENTS**
2711 Piedmont Road
Atlanta, GA 30305
Tel: 404-266-8700
Fax: 404-266-0074
More than 30,000 square
feet of architectural antiques.

**ARCHITECTURAL ANTIQUE AND SALVAGE CO. OF SANTA BARBARA**
726 Anacapa Street
Santa Barbara, CA 93101
Tel: 805-905-2446
Iron gates, grates, rails,
garden objects.

**ARCHITECTURAL ANTIQUES EXCHANGE**
715 North Second Street
Philadelphia, PA 19123
Tel: 215-922-3669
Fax: 215-922-3680
E-mail:
AAExchange@aol.com
Web site:
www.architecturalantiques.
com
Architectural salvage, leaded
and beveled glass, urns,
mirrors, street lamps, stained
glass, ironwork.

**ARCHITECTURAL ARTIFACTS**
20 South Ontario
Toledo, OH 43602
Tel: 419-243-6916
Fax: 419-243-0094
Architectural antiques, urns,
benches, statuary, iron,
columns, stained glass.

**ARCHITECTURAL ELEMENTS**
818 East 8th Street
Sioux Falls, SD 57103
Tel/Fax: 605-339-9646
Architectural antiques,
salvaged millwork, flooring.

**ARCHITECTURAL EMPORIUM**
207 Adams Avenue
Canonsburg, PA 15317
Tel: 724-746-4301
Web site:
www.architectural-
emporium.com
Architectural antiques,
stained glass, windows,
terra-cotta tiles.

**ARCHITECTURAL SALVAGE**
1215 Delaware Street
Denver, CO 80204
Tel: 303-615-5432
Architectural salvage.

**ARCHITECTURAL SALVAGE**
103 West Michigan Avenue
Grass Lake, MI 49240
Tel: 517-522-8715
Antique building materials,
beveled and stained glass.

**ARCHITECTURAL SALVAGE, INC.**
3 Mill Street
Exeter, NH 03833
Tel/Fax: 603-773-5635
Web site:
www.oldhousesalvage.
com
Windows, flooring, ironwork.

**ARCHITECTURAL SALVAGE WAREHOUSE**
53 Main Street
Burlington, VT 05401
Tel: 802-658-5011
E-mail:
salvage@together.net
Web site: www.
architecturalsalvagevt.
com
Architectural antiques,
windows, columns.

**ARCHITECTURAL SALVAGE W.D., INC.**
614-618 East Broadway
Louisville, KY 40202
Tel: 502-589-0670
Fax: 502-589-4024
Unique yard and garden
items, including statuary,
ceramics, pottery, chimney
tops, stonework,
weathervanes, ironwork,
terra-cotta, stained glass
windows, iron tables,
fountains.

**arcsal.com**
Regent House
Fore Street
Castle Cary
Somerset, England
BA7 7BG
**Tel: 01963 351797**
**Fax: 01963 351988**
E-mail: info@arcsal.com
Web site:
**www.arcsal.com**
Simple-to-use and well-illustrated Web directory of salvage, reclaimed materials, and architectural and garden antiques. All articles are sold online and delivered anywhere in the world.

**ARTIFACTS AND ANTIQUES**
105 Heady Drive
Nashville, TN 32705
**Tel: 615-354-1267**
**Fax: 615-354-0617**
E-mail:
artifacts@mindspring.com
Architectural antiques and garden ornaments.

**BARBARA ISRAEL GARDEN ANTIQUES**
296 Mt. Holly Road
Katonah, NY 10536
**Tel: 212-744-6281**
E-mail: eva@bi
  gardenantiques.com
Web site: www.
  bi-gardenantiques.com
Unique garden ornaments and furniture. SALVO Code dealer.

**THE BARNWOOD CONNECTION**
91 Bull Road
Barto, PA 19504
**Tel: 610-845-3101**
**Fax: 610-845-3167**
Used lumber.

**BELCHER'S**
2505 West Hillview Drive
Dalton, GA 30721
**Tel: 706-259-3482**
Pre-Civil War log cabins, weathered barn siding, split rails, hand-hewn beams.

**BEYOND WASTE**
3262 Wilder Road
Santa Rosa, CA 95407
**Tel: 707-792-2555**
**Fax: 707-792-2565**
E-mail: precycle@sonic.net
Web site:
www.sonic.net/~precycle
Used building materials.

**BIG SPRING PRESERVATION GROUP**
The Atrium Suites
111 North Central Avenue
Suite 5
Knoxville, TN 37902
**Tel: 423-637-2585**
**Fax: 423-637-1589**
Salvaged early log houses, log barns, outbuildings, post-and-frame barns. wood-frame houses, salvaged flooring, barn boards, windows.

**CARAVATI'S, INC.**
104 East 2nd Street
Richmond, VA 23224
**Tel: 804-232-4175**
**Fax: 804-233-7109**
E-mail:
webmaster@recentruins.
  com
Web site:
www.recentruins.com
Architectural salvage, stained-glass windows, ornamental iron, shutters, windows.

**CAROLINA ARCHITECTURAL SALVAGE AND COGAN'S ANTIQUES**
110 South Palmer Street
Ridgeway, SC 29130
**Tel: 803-337-3939**
E-mail: jcogan@usit.net
Web site:
www.usit.com/ccogan
Architectural antiques, stained-glass windows, iron fencing, iron gates.

**CHRISTOPHER HESS, INC.**
3931 Cedar Drive
Walnutport, PA 18088
**Tel: 610-760-9533**
E-mail:
chbarndawg@earthlink.net
Web site: www.
  christopherhessinc.com
Antique wood flooring and lumber.

**COLONIAL ANTIQUES**
5000 West 96th Street
Indianapolis, IN 46268
**Tel: 317-873-2727**
Architectural salvage, garden items, stained glass, hardware.

**THE EMPORIUM**
1800 Westheimer Road
Houston, TX 77098
**Tel: 800-528-3808**
**or 713-528-3808**
**Fax: 713-528-5494**
E-mail:
Emporium@NeoSoft.com
Web site:
www.the-emporium.com
Architectural antiques, gates, fountains, patio/garden urns, statuary and birdbaths, cast metal patio furniture.

**THE ENGLISH ANTIQUES WAREHOUSE**
North Carolina Highway 105
Banner Elk, NC 28604
**Tel: 828-963-4274**
**or 888-POT-TOPS**
Web site: www.
  englishantiqueimports.
  com
Architectural antiques, antique English chimneypots, farmhouse furniture, wrought-iron garden seats.

**FLORIDA VICTORIAN ARCHITECTURAL ANTIQUES**
112 West Georgia Avenue
DeLand, FL 32720
**Tel: 904-734-9300**
**Fax: 904-734-1150**
E-mail:
info@floridavictorian.com
Web site:
www.floridavictorian.com
Antique building materials, windows, flooring, doors, hardware.

**GOVERNOR'S ANTIQUES & ARCHITECTURAL MATERIALS**
8000 Antique Lane
Mechanicsville, VA 23116
**Tel: 804-746-1030**
**Fax: 804-730-8308**
Architectural antiques, iron fence gates, carved stone, statues, garden and yard furniture, slate, marble.

**HARBOR BAZAAR**
5500 Main
Lexington, MI 48450
**Tel: 810-359-5333**
Web site: www.
  tias.com/stores/bazaar
Furniture, glass.

**HARPERS BAZAAR**
263 Worcester Road
Malvern
Worcestershire, England
WR14 1AA
**Tel: 01684 568723**
**Fax: 01684 612837**
Government surplus supplier; garden and camping supplies; military, government, and industry articles and equipment.

**HORSEFEATHERS ARCHITECTURAL ANTIQUES**
346 Connecticut Street
Buffalo, NY 14213
**Tel: 716-882-1581**
**Fax: 716-882-0215**
Architectural salvage and antiques, furniture, stained glass, statuary, fencing, columns.

**KIMBERLY'S OLD-HOUSE GALLERY**
1600 Jonquill Lane
Wausau, WI 54401
**Tel: 715-359-5077**
Architectural antiques, building salvage.

**MIDWEST SALVAGE**
628 13th Avenue
Sidney, NE 69162
**Tel: 308-254-4387**
Framing and siding lumber salvaged from barns.

**THE MOBILE MERCHANT**
1052 Virginia Avenue
Indianapolis, IN 40203
**Tel: 317-264-9968**
E-mail:
mobile@antiqueresources.
  com
Web site: www.
  antiqueresources.
  com/mobile
Architectural antiques, fences, stained glass, windows.

# SOURCES

**ODOM REUSABLE BUILDING MATERIALS**
926 South Airport Road
Traverse City, MI 49686
Tel: 231-946-4883
E-mail:
reusebruce@coslink.net
Web site:
www.odomusedbuilding
materials.com
Used construction materials.

**OLDE GOOD THINGS**
124 West 24th Street
New York, NY 10011
Tel: 888-551-7333
or 212-989-8401
E-mail: feedbk@
oldegoodthings.com
Web site:
www.oldegoodthings.com
Architectural antiques,
columns, stones, stained
glass.

**OLD HOUSE PARTS CO., INC.**
24 Blue Wave Mall
Kennebunk, ME 04043
Tel: 207-985-1999
Fax: 207-985-1911
E-mail: restoration@
oldhouseparts.com
Architectural salvage,
construction materials,
windows, barn boards.

**RECYCLING THE PAST**
381 North Main Street
Barnegat, NJ 08005
Tel: 609-660-9790
Web site:
www.recyclingthepast.com
Architectural antiques, iron
gates and fencing, garden
ornaments.

**RONSONS RECLAMATION AND RESORATION**
Norton Barn
Wainlodes Lane
Norton
Gloucester, England
GL2 9LN
Tel: 01452 731236
Fax: 01452 731888
E-mail:
ronsons@netcomuk.co.uk
Web site:
ronsonsreclamation.com
Reclaimed and salvaged
materials. SALVO Code
dealer.

**SALVAGE HEAVEN**
6633 West National Avenue
West Allis, WI 53214
Tel: 414-329-7170
Fax: 414-329-7172
Architectural elements,
fixtures, furniture.

**THE SALVAGE MILL**
The Riverwalk Mill
33 South Commercial Street
Manchester, NH 03101
Tel: 603-622-0370
Fax: 603-622-0491
Architectural salvage,
windows, stained glass,
antique hardware.

**SALVAGE ONE**
1524 South Sangamon Street
Chicago, IL 60608
Tel: 312-733-0098
Fax: 312-733-6829
American and European
architectural and building
elements, garden
ornaments, art glass.

**SOUTH WEST RECLAMATION**
Gwilliams Yard
Edington
Nr Bridgwater
Somerset, England
TA7 9JN
Tel: 01278 723173
Fax: 01278 722800
Web site:
www.southwest-rec.co.uk
Reclamation dealer
specializing in flooring and
roofing tiles. SALVO Code
dealer.

**TIM & BILLY'S SALVAGE STORE**
970 Fort Wayne Avenue
Indianapolis, IN 46202
Tel: 317-632-7161
Fax: 317-632-0047
Architectural salvage, barn
boards, furniture, garden
elements.

**UNITED HOUSE WRECKING**
535 Hope Street
Stamford, CT 06906
Tel: 203-348-5371
Fax: 203-961-9472
Antiques, stained glass,
fencing, fountains, statuary.

**VERMONT SALVAGE EXCHANGE**
Gates Street
P.O. Box 453
White River Junction, VT 05001
Tel: 802-295-7616
Fax: 802-295-5744
Web site:
www.vermontsalvage.com
Architectural salvage, stone,
columns.

**WHOLE HOUSE BUILDING SUPPLY & SALVAGE**
1955 Pulgas Road East
Palo Alto, CA 94303
Tel/Fax: 650-856-0634
E-mail:
gardner@batnet.com
Web site:
www.driftwoodsalvage.
com
Salvaged building materials.

---

## WATER GARDEN SUPPLIES

**BLAKEWAY FISHERIES**
Blakeway Farm
Wedmore
Somerset
BS28 4UB
Tel/Fax: 01934 713833
Mobile: 0374 993013
Water garden supplies;
specialists in Koi carp.

**CRYSTAL PALACE PERENNIALS**
P.O. Box 154
St. John, IN 46373
Tel: 219-374-9419
Fax: 219-374-9052
E-mail: info@crystalpalace
perennials.com
Web site:
www.crystalpalace
perennial.com
Water garden supplies and
aquatic plants.

**LILYPONS WATER GARDENS**
P.O. Box 10
Buckeystown, MD 21717
Tel/Fax: 800-999-5459
E-mail: info@lilypons.com
Web site:
www.lilypons.com
Water garden supplies,
aquatic plants, fish, fish care
products.

**OASE (UK)**
P.O. Box 1709
Andover
Hampshire
SP10 3GW
Tel: 01264 333225
Fax: 01264 333226
E-mail:
oase.uk@btinternet.com
Web site:
www.oase-pumpen.com
Pumps and equipment for
water gardens.

**VAN NESS WATER GARDENS**
2460 North Euclid Avenue
Upland, CA 91784
Tel: 800-205-2425
Fax: 909-949-7217
E-mail: vnwg@vnwg.com
Web site: www.vnwg.com
Water garden supplies,
aquatic plants, fish, snails.

**THE WATERWORKS**
111 East Fairmount Avenue
Coopersburg, PA 18036
Tel: 800-360-LILY
Fax: 610-282-1262
Web site:
www.tnwaterworks.com
Water garden supplies,
aquatic plants, fish care
products.

---

## ARTISTS AND CRAFTSPEOPLE

**CANDACE BAHOUTH**
The Old Ebenezer Chapel
Pilton
Somerset
BA4 4BR
Tel: 01749 890433
Mosaic artist working in a
variety of reclaimed
materials.

**PAUL GRELLIER**
Ruriculture
Westrip Farmhouse
Cherington
Tetbury
Gloucestershire
GL8 8SL
Tel/Fax: 01452 770094
E-mail:
ruriculture@ukonline.co.uk
Web site:
www.nemonelight.com
Sculptor specializing in work
with reclaimed and salvaged
metal, stone, and wood.
Also incorporates old
agricultural and industrial
machinery and equipment
into his sculptures.

## PLANTS AND SHRUBS

**ANDRE VIETTE FARM
AND NURSERY**
P.O. Box 1109
Fishersville, VA 22939
Tel: 540-943-2315
Fax: 540-943-0782
Web site: www.viette.com
Large collection of
perennials, many unusual
plants.

**BLUESTONE
PERENNIALS**
7211 Middle Ridge Road
Madison, OH 44057
Tel: 800-852-5243
Fax: 440-428-7535
Web site:
www.bluestoneperennials.
com
Wide selection of perennials,
plants, herbs, ornamental
shrubs, bulbs,

**BUSSE GARDENS**
17160 245th Avenue
Big Lake, MN 55309
Tel: 800-544-3192
Fax: 612-263-1473
Web site:
www.bussegardens.com
More than 1,200 perennials.

**CANYON CREEK
NURSERY**
3527 Dry Creek Road
Oroville, Ca 95965
Tel: 530-533-2166
Web site:
www.canyoncreeknursery.
com
Extensive collection of
perennials, including a large
selction of fragrant violets.

**CARROLL GARDENS**
444 East Main Street
Westminster, MD 21157
Tel: 800-638-6334
Fax: 410-857-4112
Web site:
www.carrollgardens.com
Large selection of rare and
unusual plants.

**CHELSEA FARM CENTRE**
Chelsea Farm
Harp Road
Brent Knoll
Nr. Bridgwater
Somerset, England
TA9 4HQ
Tel: 01278 760480
Fax: 01278 760144
Garden and plant center.

**FORESTFARM**
990 Tetherow Road
Williams, OR 97544
Tel: 541-846-7269
Fax: 541-846-6963
Web site:
www.forestfarm.com
Large variety of perennial
plants and shrubs.

**HERONSWOOD
NURSERY LTD.**
7530 NE 288th Street
Kingston, WA 98346
Tel: 360-297-4172
Fax: 360-297-8321
Web site:
www.heronswood.com
Conifers, grasses,
perennials, shrubs, trees,
vines, collector plants.

**KURT BLUEMEL, INC.**
2740 Greene Lane
Baldwin, MD 21013
Tel: 800-248-7584
Fax: 410-557-9785
Web site:
www.bluemel.com
Bamboo, clumps, ferns,
ornamental grasses.

**LANDS END NURSERIES**
Heath House
Wedmore
Somerset, England
BS28 4UQ
Tel/Fax: 01934 713234
E-mail: landsend.bc1.net
Web site:
mikesplants@bc1.net
Wholesale garden nursery.

**NICHE GARDENS**
1111 Dawson Road
Chapel Hill, NC 27516
Tel: 919-967-0078
Fax: 919-967-4026
E-mail:
orders@nichegardens.com
Web site:
www.nichegdn.com
Wildflowers, southeastern
native plants, perennials,
ornamental grasses, trees,
shrubs.

**PLANT DELIGHTS
NURSERY**
9241 Sauls Road
Raleigh, NC 27603
Tel: 919-772-4794
Fax: 919-662-0370
E-mail:
office@plantdelights.com
Web site:
www.plantdelights.com
Unusual perennials, including
a wide variety of U.S. natives
and their Asian counterparts.

**PLANTS OF THE
SOUTHWEST**
Agua Fria Road
Route 6 Box 11A
Santa Fe, NM 87501
Tel: 800-788-7333
Fax: 505-438-8800
Web site: www.plantsofthe
southwest.com
Southwestern U.S. plants
including wildflowers,
grasses, trees, shrubs,
evergreens, vegetables,
herbs, chiles.

**POPLAR HERB FARM**
Burtle
Bridgwater
Somerset, England
TA7 8NB
Tel: 01278 723170
E-mail:
richardfish@lineone.net
Web site:
mikesplants@bc1.net
Organically grown culinary,
medicinal, and aromatic
plants; unique astrological
herb garden; herbal
preparations.

**SHADY OAKS NURSERY**
P.O. Box 708
Waseca, MN 56093
Tel: 800-504-8006
Fax: 888-735-4531
E-mail: shadyoaks@
shadyoaks.com
Web site:
www.shadyoaks.com
Hosta, perennials, grasses,
ferns, groundcovers.

**SISKIYOU RARE PLANT
NURSERY**
2825 Cummings Road
Medford, OR 97501
Tel: 541-772-6846
Fax: 541-772-4917
Web site:
www.wave.net/upg/srpn
Thousands of rare and
unusual plants from around
the world.

**WAYSIDE GARDENS**
1 Garden Lane
Hodges, SC 29695
Tel/Fax: 800-845-1124
E-mail:
info@waysidegardens.com
Web site:
www.waysidegardens.com
Unique perennials, trees,
shrubs, roses, bulbs.

**WHITE FLOWER FARM**
P.O. Box 50
Litchfield, CT 06759
Tel: 800-503-9624
Fax: 860-496-1418
Web site:
www.whiteflowerfarm.com
Wide range of annuals,
perennials, shrubs, trees,
vines, bulbs, houseplants.

# SOURCES

**WINROW NURSERIES**
Laurel Farm
Lewis Drove
Panborough
Wells Somerset, England
BA5 1PT
**Tel: 01934 712571**
**Fax: 01934 713606**
Nursery specializing in trees
and shrubs—wholesale only.

## GARDEN FURNITURE AND ACCESSORIES

**KINSMAN CO., INC.**
P.O. Box 428
Pipersville, PA 18947
**Tel: 800-733-4146**
**Fax: 215-766-5624**
Web site:
**www.kinsmangarden.com**
Garden furniture, English
ironwork planters,
accessories.

**PLOW & HEARTH**
P.O. Box 6000
Madison, VA 22727
**Tel: 800-627-1712**
**Fax: 800-843-2509**
Web site:
**www.plowhearth.com**
Garden furniture, French
planters, arbors and trellises,
accessories.

**SMITH & HAWKEN**
P.O. Box 6900
Florence, KY 41022
**Tel: 800-776-3336**
**Fax: 606-727-1166**
Web site:
**www.smithandhawken.
com**
Teak garden furniture, British
garden tools, accessories.

**SOMERSET CREATIVE PRODUCTS**
Laurel Farm
Westham
Wedmore
Somerset, England
BS28 4UZ
**Tel: 01934 712416**
**Fax: 01934 712210**
**E-mail:
somprods@globalnet.co.uk**
Authors of *Salvage Style in
Your Home* and *Salvage
Style for Outdoor Living*.
Designers and makers of
furniture and accessories
using reclaimed materials.

**WOOD CLASSICS**
20 Osprey Lane
Gardiner, NY 12525
**Tel: 845-255-7871**
**Fax: 845-255-7881**
Web site:
**www.woodclassics.com**
Garden furniture,
accessories.

## PLACES TO VISIT

**CHEEKWOOD**
1200 Forrest Park Drive
Nashville, TN 37205
**Tel: 615-353-2148**
Native plant garden, daffodil
garden, Japanese tea
garden, dogwoods, orchids,
pools, fountain, streams.

**CHICAGO BOTANIC GARDEN**
1000 Lake Cook Road
Glencoe, IL 60022
**Tel: 847-835-5440**
385 acres including an
English walled garden,
Japanese garden,
prairie garden, and aquatic
garden.

**CLEVELAND BOTANICAL GARDEN**
11030 East Boulevard
Cleveland, OH 44106
**Tel: 216-721-1600**
Floral gardens, open grassy
areas, woodlands, traditional
Japanese garden.

**DUMBARTON OAKS**
1703 32nd Street NW
Washington, DC 20007
**Tel: 202-339-6401**
Formal rose garden,
fountains, decorative stone
sculptures, cutting garden,
pebble garden, terrace
gardens.

**GOLDEN GATE PARK**
Fell and Stanyan Streets
San Francisco, CA 94117
**Tel: 415-831-2700**
Twelve garden areas
including a Japanese tea
garden, McLaren
Rhododendron Dell, 10
meadows, 14 lakes, and
680 acres of woods.

**LONGWOOD GARDENS**
U.S. Route 1
Kennett Square, PA 19348
**Tel: 610-388-1000**
300 acres of formal
gardens, conservatory
exhibits, water gardens,
topiary, fountains, flowering
trees and shrubs.

**THE LOST GARDENS OF HELIGAN**
Pentewan
St Austell
Cornwall, England
PL26 6EN
**Tel: 01726 845100**
**Fax: 01726 845101**
**E-mail: info@heligan.com**
Web site:
**www.heligan.com**

**NAUMKEAG**
Prospect Hill
Stockbridge, MA 01262
**Tel: 413-298-3239**
"Garden rooms" surround
the Naumkeag estate,
including pools, topiary,
fountains, and a Chinese
garden furnished with
Chinese sculpture.

**OLD WESTBURY GARDENS**
71 Old Westbury Road
Old Westbury, NY 11568
**Tel: 516-333-0048**
150 acres of gardens
including an English walled
garden, children's cottage
garden, and lily pond.

**TRESCO ABBEY GARDENS**
The Tresco Estate
Tresco
Isles of Scilly
Cornwall, England
TR24 0QQ
**Tel: 01720 422849**
**Fax: 01720 422807**
**E-mail:
contactus@tresco.co.uk**
Web site:
**www.tresco.co.uk**
The subtropical Tresco
Abbey Gardens, The Island
Hotel, The New Inn, Hell,
Bay Hotel (Bryher), timeshare
and holiday rental properties.

**EMMAUS HOUSE**
Clifton Hill
Clifton
Bristol, England
BS8 1BN
**Tel: 0117 907 9950**
**E-mail:
emmaushouse@msn.com**
Web site:
**www.emmaus-house.co.uk**
Conference and retreat
center. Bed and breakfast
and restaurant.

## OTHER SERVICE PROVIDERS

**BEN PIKE GARDEN DESIGNS**
Round Trees
Smallway
Congresbury
North Somerset, England
BS19 5AA
**Tel: 01934 876355**
**Fax: 01934 835566**
Garden and landscape
design, water gardens.

**BERGER PHILLIPS TOWN GARDEN DESIGN**
69 Kingsdown Parade
Bristol, England
BS6 5UG
Garden designer specializing
in urban and small-town
gardens.

**BIRTSMORTON COURT**
Birtsmorton
Malvern
Worcestershire, England
WR13 6JS
**Tel: 01684 833424**
**Fax: 01684 833837**
Corporate hospitality in a
medieval moated manor
house.

**JON GOWAN**
Aspen Cottage
Upper New Road
Cheddar
Somerset, England
BS27 3DW
**Mobile: 0585 699540**
General builder.

**SARAH GIDDENS**
**Tel: 01920 420459**
Garden designer working
throughout Southwest
England.

# INDEX

# ACKNOWLEDGMENTS

**LEFT**

A gateway to an abandoned and derelict chateau in Northern France. In any other country, the gates and pillars would probably have been "liberated" and reinstalled elsewhere.

Our thanks to all at Kyle Cathie Publishers: **Kyle Cathie, Helen Woodhall, Andrie Morris; Julia Barder, Melanie Beveridge,** our photographer **Tim Winter** and his assistant **Jo Fairclough**.

Our thanks also to the companies who generously helped us with equipment, materials, and advice:

**Black and Decker**
Hand and power tools for the professional and handyman.
**Cuprinol Ltd.**
Wood treatment products, decorative color stains, and finishes.
**Screwfix Direct**
Hardware and tools by mail order—overnight.

Also to all those who kindly allowed us to photograph their gardens:

**Susan Boss** and **Tony Hill**
**Leo** and **Jilly Cooper**
**Mr.** and **Mrs. Hubert Fear**
**Ron** and **Judy Mathews**
**Alan** and **Lucy Moore**
**Graham** and **Chrissy Price**
**John Teller** and the Ashley Vale Allotments Association
**Joe** and **Angela Tucker**
**John Woolley**

And to the following people:

**Candace Bahouth**: mosaic artist; **Sue Berger**: Berger Phillips Town Garden Design; **Nigel and Rosalie Dawes**: Birtsmorton Court; **Robert Dorrien-Smith, Mike Nelhams and Andrew Lawson**: Tresco Abbey Gardens; **Mike Duckett**: Lands End Nurseries; **Mark Durston-Sweet**: Blakeway Fisheries; **Richard Fish**: Poplar Herb Farm; **Sarah Giddens**: garden designer; **Jon Gowan**: builder; **Paul Grellier**: sculptor; **Lawrence Harper**: Harpers Bazaar; **Ron Jones**: Ronsons Reclamation and Restoration; **Thornton Kay** and **Hazel Matravers**: SALVO; **John Nelson** and **Tim Smit**: The Lost Gardens of Heligan; **Stephen Paul**: head gardener at Emmaus House; **Ben Pike**, garden designer; **Andrew Rowland**: Winrow Nurseries; **Sandra Spearing**: South West Reclamation; **Derek Wooton**: Chelsea Farm Centre Ltd.

Thanks also to Clive and Alex Limpkin for allowing us to use their garden props.